# WHAT DO I DO WHEN TEENAGERS ARE VICTIMS OF ABUSE?

Dr. Steven Gerali

 ZONDERVAN®

ZONDERVAN.com/
AUTHORTRACKER
follow your favorite authors

 youth
specialties

YOUTH SPECIALTIES

*What Do I Do When Teenagers Are Victims of Abuse?*
Copyright 2009 by Steve Gerali

Youth Specialties resources, 1890 Cordell Ct. Ste. 105, El Cajon, CA 92020 are published by Zondervan, 5300 Patterson Ave. SE, Grand Rapids, MI 49530.

ISBN 978-0-310-29195-4

*Cover design by Invisible Creature*
*Interior design by Brandi Etheredge Design*

*Printed in the United States of America*

09 10 11 12 13 14 15 • 20 19 18 17 16 15 14 13 12 11 10 9 8 7 6 5 4 3 2 1

# Contents

# What Do I Do When...
## BOOK SERIES
### | INTRODUCTION |
## Read This First!

**It's very important you read this Introduction. This series of** books has grown out of years of listening to professional and volunteer youth workers wrestle through difficult ministry situations. I usually know what's coming when the conversation starts with, "What do I do when...?" Most of the time they're looking for remedial help, but many times the issues covered in this book series have no preventive measures available. Many of these issues aren't given serious thought until they evidence themselves in the fabric of ministry. Then youth workers, church staff, parents, and even teenagers scramble to get some kind of understanding, remedy, support, or theological perspective on the situation. This series is designed to help you.

Before we move too far ahead, you need to know a few things. First, just because you read these books and acquire some helping skills, that doesn't make you a professional counselor or caregiver. In many situations you'll need to help parents and teenagers network with professional mental health workers, medical professionals, or, in some cases, legal counsel. Oftentimes the quality of care regarding these issues lies in the rapid response of helping professionals. So if you don't get anything else out of this series, get this:

The best thing you can do as an effective helper is realize you're not a trained counselor and you must refer, refer, refer.

Second, often when youth workers are in the throes of an issue, they'll quickly access the Internet for help and information. Researching something online can be very time-consuming, and it can provide unreliable information. So this book series is designed to offer reliable information that's quickly accessible for anyone who's working with adolescents.

Third, each book follows a similar format designed to help you navigate the information more easily. But more importantly, it also provides a model to help you deal with the issue at hand. What Do I Do When... books are divided into the following four sections:

## SECTION 1: UNDERSTANDING THE ISSUE, OR "PRESENTING PROBLEM"

Each book will start with an *epistemology* of the issue—in other words, the knowledge regarding its nature and scope. Many youth workers formulate their opinions, beliefs, and ideas using faulty information that's been passed through the grapevine—often without realizing the grapevine has root rot. Faulty information can change the trajectory of our actions in such a way it actually causes us to miss the mark. And many times our "misses" can be destructive to a kid who's already struggling with a painful issue.

We cannot expect to lead a teenager to the truth of Scripture if we start with a foundation that's built upon a lie or deception. We must be informed, seeking to understand the presenting problem as learners with a teachable spirit. In some cases these books may provide only the basics about an issue. But hopefully they'll be enough to create a solid foundation that gives direction for further research from reliable sources.

## SECTION 2: UNDERSTANDING HOW YOUR THEOLOGY INTERSECTS THE ISSUE OR PRESENTING PROBLEM

Each book will also cover at least one theological perspective that informs the situation. However, please note I plan to give theological insights from multiple perspectives, so you'll know the theological voices adolescents and their families hear. Some of these voices may not resonate with your particular view, but it's important you develop a gracious, loving, and understanding heart. Keep in mind you're dealing with desperate, hurting, and broken people who—in the midst of their pain and struggle—are seeking grace and hope, not someone with theological answers.

I realize there's a danger in writing like this. Whenever the playing field is leveled—in other words, when one's internalized theological framework is challenged or an opposing theological view is given—it can quickly become a fisticuffs arena to champion truth. I believe that truth brings freedom (John 8:32). But let's remember that the Pharisees believed they'd cornered the market on truth simply because they held to a rigid interpretation of the Scriptures, yet they failed to listen for God's voice in others— especially in the Messiah.

A dear friend of mine once confronted a group of students by asking, "Is your interpretation of Scripture always right?" The students knew that if they replied affirmatively, then they'd set themselves up as the source of infallibility. So they replied, "No, nobody can be right all the time."

My friend then asked, "In what areas are you wrong?"

His wisdom during that loving confrontation helped those students see that unless they openly and graciously engaged the theological perspectives of others, they'd never know if their own perspectives were lacking. Our goal in helping kids through difficult issues is to usher Christ into their situations. Many times that may not be with answers but with presence, affection, support, and understanding.

I recall a situation in which my dear, sweet, Italian mother was hurting for a young couple who'd been caught in sexual sin (she and my dad had mentored this couple). The disciplinary actions of the church were harsh and shaming. So while the church acted in rightness, it failed to see other theological perspectives that informed this situation, such as a theology of reconciliation, grace, confession, and absolution. In my conversation with my mother, I heard her engage these things because she, too, entered into the process and pain of this young couple, and she refused to apply a static template of dealing with the issue in a "right way." Instead, she decided to deal with the issue first in a loving and good way.

It's important to remember that many times rightness is not goodness. God has called his people to be good (Matthew 5:16, Ephesians 2:10, 1 Timothy 6:17-19)—not always "right." That doesn't mean we ignore truth, nor does it mean we minimize the authority of Scripture. It just means we must be incredibly and painfully careful to err on the side of that which is loving and good. Wrestling through various theological viewpoints, even if we don't initially agree with them, will keep us in the tension of being loving and good.

## SECTION 3: CONSIDERING WHAT ACTIONS WE CAN TAKE

When we understand an issue or problem, we must wrestle through the theological and consider appropriate action. That can mean anything from doing more research to aggressively seeking solutions. In this third section, I'll attempt to provide you with a framework for action, including practical examples, applications, and tips. This will only be a skeletal plan you'll need to own and tweak to fit the uniqueness of your situation. There is rarely one prescribed action for an issue—every situation is unique because of the people involved.

Throughout the years, I've watched youth workers attempt to use books about youth ministry as one uses an instruction manual for the assembly of a bicycle. They assume that if they put this screw into this hole, then this part will operate correctly. Likewise, they expect that applying a tip from a book will fix a student or situation. If only life were this easy!

Every example provided in this series of books grows out of my years of ministry and clinical experience, input from God's people, and proven results. But they're not foolproof solutions. God desires to be intimately involved in the lives of students and their families, as they trust in God through their difficult times. There is no fix-all formula—just faithfulness. So as you follow some of the directives or action steps in these books, remember you must prayerfully seek God in the resolution of the issues.

## SECTION 4: ADDITIONAL RESOURCES

In this section I'll provide some reliable resources for further help. These Internet sites, books, and organizations can assist you in mobilizing help for teenagers and their families. Hopefully this will save you many hours of hunting, so you can better invest in your students and their families.

Where needed, I'll also give a brief comment or description for the source. For example, some sources will serve to explain a different theological perspective from mainstream. This will help you to be informed before you run out and buy the book or engage the Web site.

I trust this book series will assist you in the critical care of teenagers and their families. God has put you on the front lines of attending, shepherding, and training people who are very dear and valuable to his heart. The way you respond to each person who's involved in these critical issues may have eternal consequences. My prayer is that everyone who reads these books will be empowered in a new way to usher Jesus more deeply and practically into the lives of precious teenagers.

# Understanding Abuse

## | Section 1 |

**Drew was a model junior high student—bordering on overachieving.** Bright, athletic, and ambitious, Drew connected well with his peers. He juggled a full schedule of activities well: He completed homework on time, made tennis practices and matches, was involved in church small group and youth group, and held down a job as a bagger at a local grocery store. Drew's mother, stepfather, and 10-year-old sister also were active in the ministries of First Church for the last eight years.

Drew was a part of a small group—eight junior guys who were growing spiritually and a lot of fun to be with. One day Drew asked Dan, the small group leader, to meet. Dan was surprised Drew had time to meet one-on-one. They decided to get together after small group at a fast-food restaurant for a burger and soda. "I hate it at home," Drew announced.

"Why, what's going on there?" Dan inquired.

"My step-dad and I don't get along very well," Drew replied.

"How come? I just talked to him last Sunday, and he didn't give the impression anything was wrong."

"Yeah, right!" Drew chuckled. "He's not going to tell you that he gets drunk every night and becomes a raging maniac. I hate it and I hate him," he said as he fought back tears.

"Wow! I had no idea, Drew—I'm so sorry. Has he ever hit you or hurt your mom or sister?" Dan asked with great concern.

"He punches holes in the walls and throws things. He screams profanities at all of us. I don't think he'd ever hurt my mom or sister—he has never hit them," Drew said. "But I know he scares them when he's drunk and angry because my mom and sister lock themselves in the bedroom until he passes out. I usually wait until they're safe, then I just leave."

"You leave? Where do you go?" Dan asked.

"To my friends' houses," Drew revealed. "Sometimes he does this late at night, like 2 a.m., and since my room doesn't lock, I just get out. A few nights ago I drove to the church and slept in my car in the parking lot."

"Has your mom called the police?" Dan asked.

"No. She's afraid it will make him angrier. He's fine when he's not drinking," replied Drew, pausing. "You can't let her know I told you this or tell anyone at church. If my step-dad knew that people at church know, we won't be able to come anymore—and he won't let me go to youth group."

"Is your stepdad violent with you? Has he ever hit you, Drew?" Dan asked.

Drew didn't answer for a few seconds. "No, if he did, I'd fight back."

Weeks passed and Dan continued to check with Drew and ask how his family was doing. Drew's story remained consistent. Drew treated this situation as an annoyance that disrupted the natural rhythm of family life. Whenever Dan asked if he could approach Drew's stepdad or mom to help, Drew became agitated.

Soon it was time for the youth group's winter retreat. Drew and his small group were excited about the weekend. Throughout the weekend Dan noticed that Drew was noticeably avoiding undressing in front of the other guys. This didn't seem to fit normal teenage guy behavior or Drew's past behavior. Drew would wait to change his clothes until the lights were off at night or everyone left the building, often leaving his friends waiting for him.

At one point Dan entered the cabin while Drew was changing. Dan saw lacerations, welts, and bruises on Drew's legs and back. When Dan asked Drew about these injuries, Drew admitted his stepdad had been beating him with a wire hanger. Drew was taking beatings to divert his stepdad from attacking his mom and sister.

The complexity of the situation raced through Dan's mind: News would spread through the church family...Drew's confidentiality... the financial strain the family would face if the stepdad lost his job. He wondered what he should do with a teenager who's a victim of abuse.

Most people who read this true story respond, "Dan needs to report this to child protective services." Many states mandate anyone (including volunteers) who works with minors to report suspected abuse against a minor (a subject we'll address later). Of course reporting is needed, but those who find themselves in Dan's position often don't think through carefully enough the far-reaching effects of reporting abuse. It goes far beyond simply reporting— youth workers need to go into abuse situations with their eyes wide open, ready to assist and provide long-term support.

In cases of abuse, minors may be removed from their homes, taken out of their school districts, and cut off from the church and their friends. A family may suffer financial hardships if the abuser is convicted and loses a job. While the safety of the family (especially minors) is paramount, we also must think about the sustainability of the family post-reporting. The church needs to help support both the safety and sustainability of the family.

Some may see the solution as simple while others treat the matter more delicately. I received a call from an associate pastor asking me what to do if it was suspected a teenager was being sexually abused. I probed for more specifics because appropriate solutions aren't always simple and static. The caller said there was an all-church prayer initiative in which prayer cards were made available to parishioners allowing them to write their requests and put them in offering plates.

A card came in from a 16-year-old female asking for prayer that her father would stop coming into her room at night for oral sex and intercourse. The card was unsigned.

My response was, "Pray for her—that's all you can do. She made an anonymous plea for prayer—that's what you should provide."

While this is a tragic situation, and our knee-jerk response is often to aggressively try to rescue the victim, her anonymity needed to be respected. This girl found safety in her privacy and ventured out boldly to take first steps. I advised the church to focus on training staff and creating safe environments.

Later in the conversation, the associate pastor told me the senior pastor asked the youth pastor to match the handwriting on the prayer card with other documentation he had from kids in the youth group. The youth pastor matched the card with a teen whose family was very active in the leadership of the church. The senior pastor asked the father if this was going on. At that point in the story, I interrupted the associate pastor.

"I bet the father denied the story and confessed they have been having trouble with their daughter lying, seeking attention, and behaving in hateful and destructive ways toward the family."

"Yeah, that's exactly right," the associate pastor replied.

"And I bet if the girl were confronted she would adamantly deny everything, too."

"Well, the senior pastor had the youth pastor go to her, and she denied writing the card," the associate pastor said.

As a result, this church dropped the matter with this family, choosing to believe the father's assessment of the situation.

Church leadership also concluded my approach was not proactive, so they resumed their search for the anonymous sexually abused girl.

Abuse is a complex issue and youth workers and churches need to know how to address it properly when they encounter it. Hopefully, this book will help you and your church act on abuse in appropriate ways, and bring healing and wholeness to all who are involved.

## 1.1 DEFINITION AND SCOPE

According to the U.S. Department of Justice, of the estimated 22.3 million adolescents (age 12-17) living in the United States, approximately 1.8 million have become victims of sexual abuse; 3.9 million have fallen victim to physical abuse, and almost 9 million have witnessed some serious act of violence or abuse.[1] Youth workers must be aware it's likely that teens within the scope of their ministries are or have been abused.

The Child Abuse Prevention and Treatment Act (CAPTA) states that child abuse and neglect means "at a minimum, any recent act or failure to act on the part of a parent or caregiver, which results in death, serious physical or emotional harm, sexual abuse or exploitation, or an act or failure to act which presents an imminent risk of serious harm."[2] In this act, a child is characterized as any person under the age of 18. (The age of a minor is under 18 unless the state in which the teenager resides has a different age specified by its child protection laws regarding sexual misconduct.)

Abuse can be divided into four categories: Physical abuse, emotional abuse and neglect, sexual abuse, and self-abuse. There are laws, statutes, and sentences that protect the victim from the abuser in the first three categories; in the case of self-abuse, where the abuser and victim are the same person, there is no legislation.

According to the Bureau of Justice Statistics, persons aged 12 to 24 comprise 22 percent of the population but suffer about 49 percent (2 million) of the 4.3 million serious violent victimizations.[3] In 2006 the U.S. Department of Health and Human Services' Administration for Children and Families revealed that 82.4 percent of the reported abuse and neglect cases of 12- to 17-year-olds were perpetrated by one parent acting alone or with another person; 10 percent were perpetrated by non-parental caregivers or someone responsible for the welfare of a minor (foster parents, legal guardians, unmarried partners of parents, residential treatment staff, teachers, coaches, clergy, youth group leaders, etc.).[4] It was also noted that 5.4 percent of the child abuse fatalities were among those between the ages of 12 and 17.[5] The younger the victims, the more at risk they are to being fatally wounded. These statistics are based on data collected by the child protective services in each state. Countless cases are never reported and never become part of these statistics.

Youth workers and church leaders should not assume abuse doesn't go on in their churches. The U.S. Department of Health and Human Services estimated that 3.6 million children were victims of abuse and mistreatment in 2006 alone.[6] That number is staggering.

Many teens who enter our churches and youth groups are victims, carrying a lot of pain. It's estimated that 80 percent of children who have been abused have one or more psychiatric disorders by the age of 21, including depression, anxiety, eating disorders, and post-traumatic stress disorder.[7] Children who experience child abuse and neglect are 59 percent more likely to be arrested after they become juveniles, 28 percent more likely to be arrested after they become adults, and 30 percent more likely to commit violent crime.[8]

Youth workers are on the front lines to recognize and protect teens in abusive situations. We have more life-involved contact with teens than most professionals. We see and become part of their social interactions. We do life with teens—hearing their joys, passions, concerns, dreams, and desires. We understand adolescence better than some parents because we've been around teenagers year in and year out. We watch children change and grow developmentally. We observe how they eat, sleep, talk, walk, dress. We may have a more realistic gauge on normalcy for adolescence, where others only see chaos. For all those reasons, we need to be the ones to stand in the gap for teens who are victimized.

## 1.1A DILEMMA

While all allegations and suspicion of abuse should be taken seriously, certain types of abuse (physical, emotional, and verbal) become subjective unless there is physical evidence (bruises, burns, welts, lacerations, etc.), or unless an individual witnesses the teenager being abused. **So, whenever you are in doubt, report.** It's better that child protective services discerns the situation and makes the final judgments. And by deferring to CPS, you're looking out for the best interests of the teenager and protecting yourself and your church from violating the law. With that in mind, we can still look at some factors that may create dilemmas.

**Teens can use cries of abuse as retaliatory measures.** They have the cognitive skills to know how to create conflict but lack the foresight to fully understand the consequences. For example, if they dislike the rules and restraints put on their independence by parents or caregivers, they may raise suspicions of abuse to get out of their houses. In their cognitive immaturity, they may romanticize the outcome, thinking they'll have their desired freedom.

**Some teens cry wolf out of vengeance against wrongs they believe they've suffered at the hands of caregivers.** Some accuse caregivers of abuse because they need to feel powerful and independent—or just because they want their way. Others claim they're being abused because they seek attention and enjoy others' sympathy. Teens need to be made aware that allegations of abuse, even jokingly, are very serious issues that will be dealt with appropriately. Police and government agencies get involved, and intense scrutiny is brought on the accused. Even an unsubstantiated accusation can destroy someone's reputation, career, and relationships. False accusations can also bring about legal charges and lawsuits for the accusing teen and his family.

**Some caregivers and youth workers have a difficult time discerning the difference between discipline and abuse.** As children grow into their teenage years, it becomes more difficult to know what works as disciplinary responses. Spankings are no longer an effective option, and even "grounding" may grow ineffective as teenagers advance into late adolescence. Out of frustration some parents resort to more extreme forms of physical punishment, believing it's discipline when it, in fact, borders on abuse. The following are some distinctions that may help clarify the difference:

- Discipline doesn't cause physical or emotional injury. While most abuse is evidenced by physical marks, it's also a mistake to assume that lack of injury equals no abuse. Discipline is loving, consistent, and methodical over the long haul.

- Some believe intention defines the difference between abuse and discipline. Intent to harm or not harm the teen is not the defining mark. Many abusers don't intend to harm but see their actions as extreme measures to teach unruly teens a lesson.

- Discipline is appropriate for and commensurate to the wrong that was done. If the teen fails to complete a chore, such as take out the trash, an appropriate and commensurate discipline may be to take away a privilege. An abusive response, however, would range from beatings to torturous means like standing for hours while holding the trash pail over his or her head.

- Discipline is designed to encourage moral and ethical development in a teen. This is appropriately done by establishing clear boundaries and consequences. The teen knows in advance what the outcome will be when her behavior is unacceptable. Suffering the natural consequences of an action is a disciplinary measure.

- Discipline is a consistent, loving response that considers the positive welfare of the teenager. When anything becomes more important than a teen's welfare, it can become an abusive situation.

- Discipline doesn't always mean punishment. It's a consistent "coaching" that moves the teen into adulthood as a stable, moral, socially equipped, God-honoring adult. Discipline can include a gentle correction, words of encouragement and praise, and patient support.

- Public humiliation, excessive control, torturous means, and extreme corporal punishment and force are not forms of discipline with teenagers. These are abusive measures.

**There are some cultural and religious differences in the way families discipline.** A disciplinary action may be misinterpreted as abusive by someone unaware of the culture. In an age where cultural tolerance is critical, youth workers may find themselves in the dilemma of protecting the teen and respecting a family and its cultural practices. This is a complicated dilemma because of the legal concept of *parens patriae*—parents' constitutionally protected right to raise their children and protect their children's well-being however they choose; the state can intervene only when the parents cannot or fail to meet that obligation.

**Regardless of cultural, ethnic, or religious distinctives, youth workers must first operate within the boundaries of their state's laws regarding abuse and maltreatment of minors.** If the law is vague, then there may be some wisdom in allowing the state to do its own investigation and form conclusions. An organization known as Bridging Refugee Youth and Children's Services researched state statutes to find that Colorado, Minnesota, and American Samoa (a U.S. territory) include "cultural practices" as possible exceptions to the statutory definitions of child maltreatment; other common exemptions include religious practice (30 states and one territory), corporal punishment (15 states and two territories), or poverty (seven states).[9]

In addition to understanding your state's statutes, youth workers should become aware of the cultural practices of the ethnic communities in the scope of their ministries. An accusation of alleged child endangerment can alienate a culturally different family from the ministering community of the church. This is a narrow path to walk, and it's navigated well only when the youth worker is informed by state laws and culturally normative practices. Imagine what would happen if parents dropped off their kid at youth group and left the country for vacation? Under our current laws, Joseph and Mary would've been jailed for child abuse and neglect for leaving Jesus in the temple. But according to their custom, they traveled in a caravan. The children often hung out together, and it may not have been culturally uncommon for the men to travel separately from the women. The entire caravan was responsible for the care and protection of the children. That's why Joseph and Mary didn't discover right away that their son was missing. Understanding the culture can inform us about parental practices. Conversely, it's important to note that youth workers may need to inform immigrant parents of practices deemed unacceptable in American culture. Researchers have noted some cultural differences in the discipline of teenagers.[10] One group's methods for caregiving and discipline may be another group's view of abusive or neglectful practices. For example:

- Some families that hold to fundamentalist biblical beliefs may adhere to a literal interpretation of Proverbs 13:24 which says, "He who spares the rod hates his son, but he who loves him is careful to discipline him." Consequently the teen may have welt marks from having endured the corporal punishment of a loving parent.

- Some native Caribbean families make their misbehaving teens kneel on uncooked rice as punishment for their unacceptable actions.

- Some Southeast Asian families lock their teens out of their houses for extended periods to shame them for their misbehavior and lack of respect for traditional family mores. In addition, it's shameful for them to seek refuge with other families.

- Some traditional Vietnamese families tie the ears of their misbehaving teens to doorknobs.

- In some Native American cultures, parents allow teens to run wild with little or no input as long as they feel their children's safety is not at risk. This apparent neglect is the way the culture allows their children to learn.

- The Amish community has a ritual called Rumspringa that mandates that 16-year-olds be released to experience "the outside world, flesh, and the devil" so they can make their own decision to accept the Amish faith with all its disciplines and inherit eternal life. These teenagers may be kicked out of their homes to live on their own. They're allowed to experience the world of the "English" with all its technological lures (i.e., cars, music, etc.), along with any forms of sexual practice, drug and substance use, violations of the law, etc., without parental interference. In fact, some of these Amish teens hold drunken orgies on their family properties without the intervention or interference of the family or community elders. These parties are publicized throughout the Amish world and teens from Amish communities in other states come to the party. If the teens elect to stay in their homes during Rumspringa, parents don't interfere with their chosen lifestyles.

- Some African immigrants use hot pepper as a form of discipline. The ground-up pepper is applied to the teen's eyes, mouth, or genitalia, leaving a painful burning as a disciplinary reminder (not unlike washing out a kid's mouth with soap).

- Some Asian and eastern European cultures practice "cupping" as a home remedy for their teenagers' illnesses. This practice involves putting a lit candle or a lit cotton ball soaked in alcohol on the place of the infirmity. A larger glass is put over the flame to create suction. It is believed this suction draws the illness out of the body. The practice often leaves burns or a ring-shaped welt.

- Folk medicine, still practiced by some Asian families, involves pinching, scraping, or rubbing raw an area of infirmity with a coin or solid object.

- Some families have faith practices that prohibit the use of medicines and medical involvement. While many states have laws regulating this practice, it still occurs.

- Some Latino families practice Santeria, a ritualistic remedy for illness, emotional problems, or life stressors. Santeria means "the way of the saints" and is a blend of pagan superstitions, African Orisha worship (or spiritism), and Catholic and Protestant traditions. Santeria involves the application of potions made from plants and the blood or entrails of sacrificed animals. The teen is made to keep the potions and blood/entrails on his body in expectation of a healing miracle. The foul-smelling concoction and lack of contemporary medical care can appear neglectful and abusive—especially if the teen dislikes the practice.[11]

## 1.1B MYTHS ABOUT TEEN ABUSE

Many myths regarding abuse can keep teenagers from receiving the care they need. Some of these myths can also have a destructive effect and negatively influence the mission of the church to youth. Let's examine some of those myths:

**MYTH #1: Abuse only happens in urban communities and lower-income homes.** Abuse is no respecter of persons. It cuts across ethnic and socioeconomic lines. Commonly, families are at a higher risk for abuse when they experience a lot of stress resulting from shifts in economic or moral lifestyles, marital disharmony, chronic illness or loss, or lack of strong social networking and support from extended family and friends. Families with a history of violence and substance abuse also present a greater risk.

**MYTH #2: Teenagers bring abuse on themselves.** While living with a teen can be trying, stressful, and unnerving, no individual deserves abuse. Abuse is a controlled, repeated action. Abuse rarely happens because of a teen's behavior. Most of the time the abuse has been going on for a long time, beginning when the teen was a child. Adults need to remember they are older, wiser, more experienced, and responsible to act appropriately. If parents believe that their teens are pushing them beyond the breaking point, they should seek help. There's a wealth of resources available to parents, from books to counseling or social services. Most school counselors have resources available for parents and other caregivers who feel overwhelmed.

**MYTH #3: Abuse—more specifically sexual abuse—only happens to females.** Many people believe that teenage guys have the means to protect themselves in abusive situations, but they fail to see that a larger factor in abuse is psychological, centering on intimidation and control. Many teenage guys are not at a place in their cognitive development to discern the psychodynamics of a situation. As a result, though they may be physically strong, they're overpowered because of their immature cognition.

In the case of sexual abuse, because we live in a culture that elevates male sexual virility, and because sexual virility is predicated on the notion a guy can and should be getting sex anytime, anywhere, and any way, many believe that a guy cannot be sexually abused (we'll discuss this in more detail later in the book). Rather, we must understand that teenage guys are vulnerable to all kinds of abuse—including sexual abuse.

**MYTH #4: Teenagers are old enough, smart enough, and resourceful enough to overcome abusers.** While teens may appear physically virile, energetic, strong, capable, and adultlike, they're not adults. Often when the abuse of a teen is exposed, the question is asked, "Why didn't you just leave?" or "Why didn't you just push them away?" In Drew's story, he said that if his stepdad hit him, he would hit him back. But the truth is that Drew never fought back—he felt trapped because he lacked the skills and maturity to be autonomous and to seek any kind of help. While teenage bodies are growing into adult forms, teens' intellectual and emotional development may not increase at the same rate.

One of the primary tasks of adolescence is growing into autonomy. Teens are struggling through this task, learning who they are, how they fit into the world, what contributions they make to those around them, and how they can break from primary caregivers to live productive adult lives. But because teens haven't navigated through the murky waters of adult independence, they can be easily intimidated, emotionally vulnerable, and psychologically manipulated—especially by those in authority. On the outside they may look fully grown and capable of stopping abuse, but internally teens are more like children than adults.

**MYTH #5: Teenagers are most often abused by strangers.** The rise of Internet relationships has made teenagers more accessible to strangers and vulnerable to being victimized by them. But the overwhelming majority of teenage abuse happens at the hands of those they know and have a relationship with. Most common are family members, friends, and dating partners. Many times these abusers hold some form of power or authority (real or perceived) over their victims.

**MYTH #6: Abused teenagers show physical signs of injury.** While there are behavioral and psychological signs and symptoms of abuse (we"ll examine these later in the book), there may not be any physical signs. Teens in abusive situations, unlike children, learn to hide their physical wounds with clothing and/or makeup. Bruises and injuries may also be easily explained and excused because teens are often involved in physical activities (sports, exercise, and horseplay). Teens also hide and suppress emotional wounds as they immerse themselves in friendships and dating, pop culture, and at-risk behaviors such as drug and alcohol experimentation.

**MYTH #7: Abused teenagers are more prone to becoming abusers.** I've had the opportunity to chair the departments of youth ministry and adolescent studies at three different Christian schools. Students in my programs were required to serve in local churches each semester and complete an internship during their last year. We encouraged students to develop strong relationships with their churches before it came time to do internships. One of my students named Chris served in a youth ministry for two years prior to his senior year. The youth pastor at his church was glad to have Chris serving and often verbalized to me how significant Chris' contribution was in the lives of teens and the youth ministry program. About two months into Chris' internship year, the church decided to have all youth and children's ministry workers complete an application in order to have them on file. One question on the application was, "Have you ever been physically or sexually abused?" Chris had never before disclosed (not even to his closest friends and some family) that he was sexually abused repeatedly as a child by a babysitter. But he decided to be candid and share his past on the application. When the senior pastor read this, he immediately dismissed Chris from working in the youth ministry. The senior pastor believed that people who've been abused become abusers. The pastor was unmoved in regard to his decision—even after the youth pastor and the university came to Chris' defense. The situation escalated, and the youth pastor's employment was in jeopardy, too, because he advocated for Chris.

Chris was humiliated and damaged by this—his secret now became like a scarlet letter. The humiliation of being removed from ministry and banned from having contact with minors was so great that Chris left school in the middle of the term. Soon neither the university, his friends and roommates, nor his family knew where Chris was and feared something terrible had happened to him.

Two weeks later Chris came back and got counseling to help heal from the victimization of his childhood abuse and the wounding injustice he faced from church leadership.

While many incarcerated abusers report having been abused,[12] this doesn't mean we can conversely conclude that about all abuse victims. The church should be a sanctuary for the abused, a place to find healing, hope, and wholeness. A myth like this has a very destructive effect that perpetuates pain for people who've been abused.

MYTH #8: Abused teenagers are damaged or impaired for the rest of their lives. Some mental health professionals and schools of thought follow this notion, treating past abuse as an inflicted disability (similar to the loss of a limb) where the victim must learn to rise above his infirmities. Any dysfunction in the victim's life may be the result of repressed memories that can be traced back to the abuse.

Without question the horror and trauma of abuse have deep effects on its victims. But I believe that God desires restoration and healing in all people. The church is God's agent in the world to bring God's wholeness to victims of abuse. If we hold to a view that places people as perpetual victims, we don't embrace the fullness of God's power and intent to restore and reconcile us. Jesus liberates victims from the effects of their victimization.

We need to bring hope into the lives of teenage abuse victims, believing that the God of the Bible is bigger than any trauma that teens will ever experience.

**MYTH #9: Sexually abused teens are more likely to develop same-sex orientations or become sexually deviant.** Some believe homosexuality is the result of abuse by someone of the same sex. Not only is this unsubstantiated, the opposite is true: Most gay men and women have never been abused.[13] To assume most abuse victims turn into sexual deviants is also unsupported. (Later in this book we'll show that some sexual-abuse victims act out sexually in an attempt to normalize their experiences, but this is different from developing deviant lifestyles.)

**MYTH #10: Perpetrators are creepy, angry perverts with mental disorders.** In 2007 the U.S Department of Health and Human Services found that 86 percent of all child abusers were parents or family members (80 percent were parent(s); 6.6 percent were other family members) and that 56.5 percent of the perpetrators were women while 42.4 percent were men.[14] More than half were charged with neglect while 10 percent physically abused and 7 percent sexually abused. Of the nonfamily sexual abusers, almost 58 percent were friends and neighbors and the rest were known by the victim (i.e., teachers, coaches, day-care workers, etc.).[15] The American Psychological Association also notes that comparatively, most perpetrators of sexual child abuse aren't strangers—they're known by their victims.[16] This means that many who abuse children and teens look like you and me, live on our streets, and attend our churches. They are most often not random people, but rather people we know who are invested in society and already have a relational connection with a teen.

## 1.2 PHYSICAL ABUSE

Physical abuse is force (e.g., hitting, beating, biting, shoving, assault with a weapon, burning, shaking, or any other attempt to cause bodily injury) exerted against a person. If you research teenage physical abuse, you'll probably find lots of material on bullying and violence outside the home.[17] Though less propagated, many teens suffer from physical abuse and violence in their homes. Sometimes a teenager can become the punching bag for parents in marital discord. The normal developmental fight for autonomy and teenage rebellion is difficult for everyone—even healthy parents. So for parents dealing with pain, normal teen angst appears as an affront and is often interpreted as a personal attack. As a result, hurting parents may make their teens the objects of upset—and the cause of their issues.

## 1.2A FAMILY VIOLENCE

Family violence is broken into three categories: Spousal abuse (sometimes called domestic violence or intimate partner violence), child abuse, and elderly abuse. Most of the information on family violence centers on spousal abuse. In 2005 the Department of Justice reported that family violence accounted for 11 percent of all violence between 1998 and 2002; 49 percent of those offenses were directed against spouses, and 11 percent involved parents attacking their children.[18] In addition, most of the data on child abuse in domestic settings centers on children under the age of 13. This may mean that children are victims of family violence more than teenagers—or that teenage victims of family violence don't report it, or it goes undetected, or that teenagers are more likely to escape being victims of family violence than younger children or spouses.

The American Bar Association (ABA) found a significant correlation between spousal and child abuse, estimating that 30 percent to 60 percent of families who experience abuse experience both kinds of abuse.[19] The longer the spousal abuse occurs, the more likely children or teens in the family are at risk. Teens are more likely to become victims of physical abuse when they intervene on behalf of parents or younger children who are being abused, as was the case with Drew, who often escaped his stepfather's violence because he could walk or drive away from home. While most teenagers have a level of autonomy in which they have no problem leaving the house temporarily, younger children most often don't feel safe leaving home. Older teens may also have a car available, making it easier to avoid domestic violence.

The physical abuse of a teenager can include

- Excessive slapping, hitting, or punching.
- Burning—often with scalding water or cigarettes.
- Beatings, which can include kicking, shoving, and choking.
- Assault with a weapon or firearm. Weapons can include wire hangers, sticks, bats, belts, bottles, pipes, knives, etc.

## 1.2B SIGNS AND SYMPTOMS OF PHYSICAL ABUSE

Some signs that would indicate a teenager is being physically abused include:

**Recurring and unexplained injuries.** Bruises, cuts, lacerations, welts, bald patches on scalp, bite marks, black eyes, or burns. The teen may make bizarre or illogical explanations for these injuries.

**Clothing that may be inappropriate for the season.** Long-sleeved shirts, high necklines, and long pants in the summer cover injuries. If kids suddenly change their clothing styles as a means of covering themselves (e.g., wearing excessive make-up or adopting uncharacteristic styles such as punk, gangsta, combat, or Goth), this may also be an alert.

**Refusal to dress or undress for gym class, on retreats, etc.** This should be gauged with the consideration that some teens are very modest or within the scope of normal teenage behavior.

**Pulling away from physical contact or cowering when someone suddenly comes in close contact.**

**Becoming very fearful and panicking when it's suggested a parent (possible abuser) be contacted to help understand their injuries.** When contacted, a parent or guardian who is abusing may explain the injuries as careless adolescent behaviors, give unconvincing answers, or may propose a different reason from the one the teen gave.

**Impaired movement.** Difficulty breathing, walking, sitting, lying down, standing after they've been seated, or impaired range of motion in arms, torso, or legs. Abdominal injuries may cause vomiting and swelling. Teens may protect the injured areas by covering them with their arms or holding their stomach, etc. Head injuries may result in dizziness, blackouts, and headaches.

**Changing behavior to ward off attention and suspicion of physical injury.** This could include a teen suddenly becoming an overachiever or class clown. Underachieving tendencies such as slacking on responsibilities, a drop in school performance, showing recklessness, and disinterest may also be a mask to hide pain.

**Engaging in risky or dangerous behaviors in order to explain injuries.**

**Becoming more aggressive, angry, and violent.**

**Changes in mood and temperament.**

**Running away from home.** The National Runaway Switchboard reports that 1.6 to 2.8 million teenagers run away from home each year, and that teens between the ages of 12 and 17 are at a higher risk of homelessness than adults. The overwhelming impetus for teens to run away is conflict with their parents and physical and sexual abuse.[20]

## 1.2C PHYSICAL DATING VIOLENCE

According to the U.S. Centers for Disease Control, one teen in eleven experiences some form of abuse in dating relationships.[21] Other studies suggest that a little more than three of ten teens (33 percent) report experiencing some form of abuse in their dating relationships, of which 12 percent experience some form of physical violence.[22] Discrepancies in these statistics probably stems from the fact that there's no agreed-upon definition of dating abuse (some define it as being hit by a dating partner whiles others refer to it as any physical harm). All told, about a third of teenage dating relationships experience some form of physical aggression.[23] No matter how you look at these statistics, dating violence is not uncommon and may even be happening within our youth ministries.

Commonly referred to as Physical Dating Violence (PDV), dating violence can include sexual assault and date rape, physical assault and battery, and psychological abuse, including manipulation, control, and verbal misconduct and threats. Consider the following facts:

- Teen dating violence cuts equally across genders. Approximately one in ten females and one in eleven males (9.8 percent of females; 9.1 percent of males) report being physically hurt by a boyfriend or girlfriend.[24] The psychological suffering and fear resulting from physical abuse is greater on females. Males who report being hurt by their girlfriends minimize the hurt and pass off the attacks as amusing.[25] Yet 8 percent of these males and 9 percent of these females report having been to a hospital emergency room for an injury inflicted by a dating partner.[26]

- Dating violence affects all ethnicities. The highest reported rates are among black adolescents (13.9 percent), followed by Latino adolescents (9.3 percent) and white (7.0 percent) adolescents.[27]

- Victims of dating abuse are also more likely to engage in at-risk behaviors such as binge drinking and substance abuse, physical altercations, sexual activity, and suicide attempts.[28]

- Victims of dating violence often misread and dismiss the behaviors of their abusive partners as deep, jealous love. Some may fear losing their relationships, so they shoulder the blame for the abuse, thinking they deserved this treatment. Concurrently, the offenders usually place blame for their abusive behaviors on their victims.

- Abusers often control their victims. They may tell the victim what clothes he should wear, whom he can or cannot talk to, where he can and cannot go, etc. The victim's privacy is constantly being violated and his whereabouts are being monitored. Abusers believe they have the right to invade conversations their victims are having with friends and family, have password access to their victims' emails, and monitor their social network sites, phone calls, and text messages.

- Abusers tend to "techno-stalk" their partners—texting or calling repeatedly, from 10 to 30 times an hour, to keep tabs on their partners.

- Abusers tend to be extremely jealous, have anger issues, exhibit unpredictable mood swings, adhere to very rigid masculine or feminine roles, and can be hypersensitive. Their behaviors escalate during disagreements to the point where they believe they must use force to underscore that they're right.

- Abusers tend to control their partners by making threats (e.g., physical harm, death, suicide of the abusers) if the victims ever decided to break up or report the abuse to those in authority.

- Abusers may coerce their partners into unwanted sexual situations. The victims may willingly engage in sexual acts as a way to avoid more drama or dire consequences.

- Female abusers tend to use verbal and psychological means to mistreat their dating partners. They manipulate, threaten, and humiliate by using technology (e.g., posting vicious, embarrassing rumors about everything from their partners' clothing choices to sexual orientation).

- Teens in same-sex dating relationships are equally likely to experience violence as those in opposite-sex relationships.[29]

- Abusive females may become abusive to their partners' brothers or fathers (often behind their back), and abusive males do the same to their partners' sisters and mothers.

- Abusers may make unwanted sexual advances. This can range from coercive measures, such as telling victims to prove their love, to threats. Often date rape is the result of this abusive behavior. These unwanted sexual advances also can include pressure to become sexually active, not use protection in an existing sexual relationship, or (among some women abusers) seeking to become pregnant in order to keep their partners.

- While verbal and emotional abuse may happen in public, most physical dating abuse takes place in one of the homes of the couples. Most abusers can be controlled enough to wait and take their anger out later when they're alone with their partners. This often catches the victims off guard and keeps the physical abuse secret.

## 1.2D SIGNS AND SYMPTOMS OF PHYSICAL DATING VIOLENCE

Some signs that teens may be in abusive dating relationships include

- Spending an unusual (almost unhealthy) amount of time together with a boyfriend or girlfriend, apart from friends and family.
- Obsessively, secretly, and urgently responding to text and phone messages.
- Withdrawing or isolating from friends and family.
- Changes in mood and temperament (e.g., a happy, outgoing person becomes aloof, pensive, and sad).
- Being easily panicked or fearful.
- Frequent truancy from school and becoming irresponsible.
- Shift in school performance and a drop in grades.
- Physical signs of injury.
- Experimentation, use, or abuse of substances as a means of escape.

- Suicide attempts. Those in violent dating relationships often feel trapped and believe the only way out is to take their own lives.

## 1.3 EMOTIONAL ABUSE

Emotional (psychological) abuse is broad in scope and can be difficult to assess. Commonly it falls into three categories: Verbal abuse, neglect, and overcontrol. Emotional abuse often erodes teens' self-esteem and sense of value and is a threat to their emotional well-being. Abused teens may believe they're worthless and that nobody could love or desire them. Many times they'll push people away just to avoid the "inevitable" rejection they've come to expect. Emotional abuse can involve threatening or terrorizing, withholding love and attention, public humiliation, exposure of private or embarrassing information, intimidation, guilt tripping, manipulation or coercion, and isolating the teen.

The emotional or psychological abuse of teenagers has a direct bearing on and impairment of their development. Here are some of the effects:

- Developing teens are very body- and image-conscious. Berating their appearance and abilities can create a complex carried into adulthood. The awkwardness of physiological changes automatically makes them feel abnormal; it's worsened when abusive parents or caregivers shame, draw attention to, or authoritatively deem teens abnormal—this can shape their self-esteem toward the belief they're worthless.

- Developing teens are exercising cognitive skills that allow them to think in advanced adult stages and formulate personal values. Emotional abusers manipulate and "brainwash" their victims by telling them what to think, read, watch, etc. Teens often become convinced they're stupid and that their thoughts are unimportant. In addition teens may begin to believe that their experiences are normal and that they're always to be in subordinate or victimized roles.

- Developing teens discover and formulate their identities and develop autonomy. Abusers control their victims by preventing them from discovering, questioning, or exploring their talents, abilities, and innate qualities. Often teen victims of emotional abuse are controlled to the point where they're "not allowed" to spend time with friends, seek application to colleges, or do anything that may result in accolades or attention. Teen victims may also become intent on pleasing their abusers (a task that can never be achieved). This tends to take all their energy and robs them of developing the social skills necessary to have quality relationships.

- Developing teens are at a critical faith-formative stage. They're beginning to own and understand their faith, and their circumstances may not gel with the teaching of a loving God—a God who rescues. Many teens begin to believe they're the exception to God's rules and promises—particularly if they sense their prayers aren't being answered. Helping an abused teen understand his identity in Christ is often an uphill battle against distorted, threatening, tangible messages that have been reinforced daily for many years.

## 1.3A VERBAL ABUSE

Teenagers are in identity development—they're beginning to understand who they are. Much of the data they use to formulate their self-image comes from the messages they receive from family, friends, other significant adults, media, and society. The more prominent that individuals are in teens' lives, the more powerfully those persons are in shaping teens' identities. In short, words are powerful.

Therefore when teens are constantly verbally assaulted by parents or caregivers, they begin to internalize identities of worthlessness.

Verbal abuse is often evidenced in the following ways:

- Abusers repeatedly disapprove of teen victims, refusing to accept anything they do as good enough. This often spirals into a destructive cycle in which teens obsessively attempt to win the approval of their abusers, even in the midst of continual verbal assaults.

- Criticizing and always pointing out what's not right. This can be subtle and even appear as though the abusers are trying to help their teen victims improve or behave rightly. They constantly point out flaws or what "could have been" rather than championing and praising the teens' best efforts. Teens in these cases often begin to believe they're failures who can never do anything right.

- Embarrassing and humiliating teens in front of their peers. This often includes deliberately coming to places where teens are socializing (e.g., school, friends' homes, sporting activities, etc.) and making a scene at the expense of the teens. Technology has provided more avenues for this abusive practice. Parents or caregivers can post embarrassing information or expose faults on social networking sites.

- Deliberately starting arguments and fights with teens. The abusers seek to blame, find faults with, or pick on teens until an argument occurs. They usually try to make their victims feel responsible for the negative feelings the abusers are experiencing and berate them for being belligerent, oppositional children. Many times teens in these situations feel trapped because they know that when they come in contact with the abusers, they'll be attacked or arguments will ensue, even if the teens work desperately to avoid it. This often causes teens to run away from home.

- Lying and sarcasm. Abusers may manipulate the truth and continuously be sarcastic to control their victims. They may concoct stories to get teens to disclose information, lie about their teens' friends, etc. Some verbally abused teens may also mimic this behavior to get their way or manipulate others.

- Screaming. Abusers often scream and yell hysterically. This tactic intimidates and embarrasses teenage victims. Sometime abusers yell and scream, accompanied with violent acts such as punching holes in the wall and breaking or throwing objects, etc. While the violence isn't directed at their victims, it keeps them fearful it may visit them at some point.

## 1.3B NEGLECT

Teens have more autonomy than younger children, making it more difficult to assess if teens are being neglected. The neglect of teenagers can include:

- Withholding, compromising, or failing to give the quality of care essential to teens' growth and survival (e.g., not providing food, shelter, clothing, medical treatment, education, etc.).

- Failing to place limits on teens (i.e., allowing them to behave any way they desire).

- The silent treatment: Refusing to give guidance to and acknowledge teenagers.

- Kicking teens out of the house to live on the street. Half of homeless teens reported that their parents either kicked them out of their homes or knew they were leaving because of conflicts and didn't care.[30] Eighty percent of teenage girls on the street or in shelters reported being sexually or physically abused prior to leaving home. In addition 34 percent of all runaway teens (guys and girls) reported being sexually abused before leaving home, and 43 percent reported being physically abused.[31]

- Most of the time neglect is preceded by another form of abuse. The most common endangerment component reported by 70 percent of all runaway teens is physical or sexual abuse—or the fear of abuse upon returning home.[32]

- Any behavior by parents or caregivers that puts teenagers in harm's way can be deemed neglect. This includes not going after or reporting runaway teens, transporting teens while intoxicated, providing illegal substances for teens, etc.

- Often neglected teens keep up charades that everything is all right by bouncing between friends' homes. They don't want their friends' parents to catch on for fear they'll be sent back home. When they run out of options, teens find shelter in their cars, abandoned buildings, parks, under bridges, or on rooftops.

- The longer neglected teens are away from proper care, the more at risk they are to danger. Many are forced to drop out of school, become abducted, even sold into sexual slavery; they also may fall into sordid social circles, seeking acceptance and protection, and are more likely to be victims of assault or homicide, engage in illegal activity, become addicted to drugs and alcohol, and commit suicide.

## 1.3C OVERCONTROL

Over-controlling parents often believe they're protecting or exercising age-appropriate discipline with their teenagers. Often controlling parents feel extreme distrust of and the need to exercise unusual control over their teens. When adolescence begins (about age 12), the natural tendency is to begin pulling away from parents. This is essential for the teens' healthy identity development, formation of essential life skills, and finding autonomy. Teens can do this under the watchful eyes of parents or caregivers, but this becomes abusive when adults put their needs, fears, desires, and plans ahead of their children's well-being.

The turn of the 21st century yielded a new type of parent—the "helicopter parent." This term has been assigned to parents who hover over their children, micromanaging their lives, making their decisions, fighting their battles, interfering in the natural consequences of their teens' behavior, resolving their conflicts, and meddling in their relationships. Helicopter parents' unhealthy behavior is most often revealed during their child's teen years, when their controlling ways are glaringly not age-appropriate for their sons and daughters. Many, especially those in the evangelical faith, have presented this parenting style as good and acceptable, justifying it as a parent's right and responsibility to be actively involved in their children's lives. Helicopter parents are quick to point to "neglectful" parents as the warped standard of parenting today. While parental involvement is necessary to raise healthy children, helicopter parents border on and often cross the line of being overcontrolling—which is a form of abuse. Some overcontrolling, abusive behaviors can include:

- Reading their teens' emails and posing as their teens in chat rooms or on instant messages to get information from friends. These parents may also become demanding and controlling of their teens' friends.

- Meddling in the plans and social contexts of their teens. They may constantly call their teens to identify their whereabouts, show up at places where they expect their teenagers to be, make their teens' plans, or even attempt to make the plans for their teens' friends by calling other parents and manipulating them. This is often humiliating to the victims and trivial to the parents, who tend to believe that their teens are incapable of making good choices or decisions. Any feelings of humiliation are viewed as a childish response the teens will outgrow.

- Removing bedroom doors so the teens have no privacy. Some parents are so afraid their teens may be sexually active, engage in masturbation, or do other unacceptable things that they create environments where they can always monitor their teens' behaviors. Some parents may also demand that bathroom doors be left slightly ajar for the same reasons. Abusive, controlling parents believe that their fears give them the right to violate their teens' privacy and keep them in abnormally submissive states.

- Dominating. Some parents exhibit abusive control by regimenting everything their teens do, including telling them what they should wear (laying out their clothes each day), when and what they should eat, where they should be at all times, and whom they can or cannot socialize with. This is different from helping teens choose good friends; controlling parents may say, "You can't talk to Susan today; she takes up too much of your time, and you already talked to her yesterday."

- Always being right. This is often coupled with parents constantly belittling their teens. This may be played out with the abusers deliberately doing the opposite of what their teens want or need.

- Minimizing their teens' feelings. If teens express emotion, their abusers often use that as an opportunity to keep their teens oppressed. Comments such as "Grow up and quit crying like a baby" or, "You're so childish," etc., are examples of minimizing feelings.

- Unpredictable responses. Outbursts of rage, hate, delight over the teens' misfortune, etc., are examples of the unpredictability abusers use to keep teens under control. These responses can keep teenagers in fear and confusion and make them feel worthless.

- In the teens' late adolescence these parents may seek access to their sons' or daughters' college records to monitor every class. They also may create schedules for their children so they know where they are every moment of the day (they'll often call 15 to 20 times a day to make sure their late adolescents are where they should be), monitor their social activities by demanding phone numbers and access to friends so they can keep closer tabs, select and register for their children's courses, and demand and gain access to their emails and private communications (including monitoring their phone calls by accessing itemized call records.) They may frequently come to the university to cook, clean, and do their late adolescents' laundry—along with a host of other unthinkable, inappropriate, controlling behaviors.

## 1.3D SIGNS AND SYMPTOMS OF EMOTIONAL ABUSE

Some signs and symptoms that teens may be emotionally abused include:

**Self-abasement.** Teens may refer to themselves as stupid, ugly, worthless, etc. These comments usually surface when teens make mistakes, are asked to do something, or when others are being talked about in positive ways. The more pronounced the emotional abuse, the more frequent and intense the self-abasement. This can also take the form of the teens believing and verbalizing they deserve the abuse, pain, or negative experiences life affords them.

**Timidity. Feeling and acting powerless.**

**Constant fear, depression, or feelings of humiliation and shame.**

**Lying to protect themselves.** They say what they think others want to hear rather than what they truly think, feel, did, etc. This can also include fabricating stories in hopes people will accept them (e.g., claiming to know famous people, owning things they don't own, accomplishing feats that never happened, etc.).

**Trouble accepting compliments.** Positive comments may be so foreign to these teens that their reactions range from passing it off, disagreement, or accusing others of lying to them.

**Constantly seeking approval and acceptance,** though they may feel as though they don't know what it feels like, or if they'll ever gain it.

Overreacting to their mistakes either with self-anger, rage, or fear of reprisal.

Exhibiting some regression in maturity or an inability to developmentally mature in cognition, social skills, or spiritual development.

Indecision and inability to make informed decisions.

Overwhelming attitudes of defeat and passivity.

Engaging in self-harm (cutting, branding, etc.). This may include use of, abuse of, or experimentation with substances, as well as suicide ideation or attempts.

Inability to perform normal life skills appropriate to adolescence. This may include extreme social awkwardness.

Signs and symptoms of neglect can include:

- Changes in physiology, including weight loss, appearing gaunt, fatigue, and ravaging hunger. Teens may express constant hunger beyond what's normal for adolescence and in a way that gives the impression there's been a lack of food rather than a craving for food.
- Poor hygiene from lack of toiletries, places to shower, etc. This may expose the fact that neglected teens aren't living in their homes. They may also come to school, church, or other places where they can use public showers.
- Tattered, unkempt, dirty clothes. They may also ask their friends if they can borrow clothes.
- Constant asking to borrow money.
- Scavenging and hoarding behaviors.

- Engaging in survival sex. This is a form of prostitution out of desperation to eat, have shelter and clothing, and make some money. For males this results almost exclusively in gay encounters. Straight teenage guys willingly engage in homosexual sex with older men as a means of survival. This is often referred to as "gay for pay."
- Untreated or ignored medical problems.
- Dropping out of school or being gone or missing for long periods of time.
- Shift in social circles. Teens on the streets tend to find camaraderie with others in similar circumstances.

## 1.4 SEXUAL ABUSE

The U.S. Department of Health and Human Services Administration for Children and Families defines sexual abuse[33] as:

A. the employment, use, persuasion, inducement, enticement, or coercion of any child to engage in, or assist any other person to engage in, any sexually explicit conduct or simulation of such conduct for the purpose of producing a visual depiction of such conduct; or

B. the rape, and in cases of caretaker or inter-familial relationships, statutory rape, molestation, prostitution, or other form of sexual exploitation of children, or incest with children.

The term *child* refers to a person under the age of 18. Some state laws differ on what age constitutes a minor. One modification made from state to state regarding age parameters has to do with a minor who sexually abuses a younger minor. For example, this means that a 16-year-old who has sexual contact with a 10-year-old can be charged with sexual abuse. States vary their statutes in regard to the number of years between perpetrators and victims (it can range from three to five years). In addition, if a 19-year-old is sexually involved with a 17-year-old, this could constitute sexual abuse.

Sexual abuse is any sexual contact between an adult and a minor, even if the minor consents. Teenage sexual abuse can include:

- Engagement in sexual situations.
- Exhibitionism: When adults expose their genitalia to teens or engage in sexual acts in front of them.
- Fondling teens' genitalia. This could also include frotteurism, which is the act of rubbing one's genitalia against an unsuspecting, nonconsenting person.
- Having oral-genital contact.
- Digital penetration. The use or insertion of a finger to stimulate or penetrate the vagina or anus.
- Rape. It ranges from forced intercourse (or forced sexual acts) to statutory rape (as in the case of a 17-year-old consenting to have sex with a 19-year-old).
- Sodomy. This term is more commonly used for genital-anal sex but can also refer to forced same-sex acts, both oral and anal.
- Showing teens pornographic material or using them to make pornographic material.
- Masturbation with, by, or of teenagers.
- Incest. Any sexual contact or engagement with family members.
- Prostitution or sexual slavery. The U.S. Department of Justice estimates 293,000 American youth are currently at risk of becoming victims of commercial sexual exploitation.[34] The majority are runaways and neglected teens.
- Sexual molestation.
- Voyeurism. When teens are forced to touch, fondle, or engage in sexual acts while perpetrators watch.

If any child or minor (up to age 18) is the target of a person's sexual urges or desires, that person is commonly referred to as a *pedophile*. If a pubescent, early adolescent (age 10-14) is the target of a person's sexual urges and advances, that person is more specifically known as a *hebephile*. If a middle or late adolescent (age 14-18) is the target of a person's sexual urges and advances, that person is known specifically as an ephebophile. According to a U.S. Department of Justice report, 67 percent of all reported sexual abuse victims are under the age of 18, with 12- to 17-year-olds encountering the most sexual abuse of any age range.[35]

Teens who are sexually abused don't often disclose it because of the guilt and shame associated with the nature of their victimization. Unfortunately those who've stumbled into sexual sin, are sexual abusers, or are victims may not see the church as a safe place to find help. Churches often communicate that sexual sin is the worst of all offenses, vocalizing anger and condemnation, with few signs of acting graciously and restoratively to people victimized by or perpetuating sexual sin. Teens are taught that lost virginity and sexual sin carries irreversible, lifelong relational repercussions. Too often church leaders have made the consequences of sexual sin seem greater than the scope of God's restorative, atoning grace.

Please understand me. I believe that teens need to be challenged to live sexually pure lives. I believe abstinence should be taught to our teens. My concern is that fear seems the primary motivator in this message. We fear that if we teach teens God is gracious and restores broken sexuality they'll run out and have sex. Books that teach teens to avoid dating because of the lustful luring of sex that accompanies it have been turned into bestsellers. Teens are told their (God-given) sexual drives are lust battles every person must conquer. By perpetuating fear and avoidance of understanding our sexuality, we propagate shame in the lives of our teens.

It's hard to imagine that approximately one in four girls and one in six guys sitting in our churches live with the overwhelming secret that they are frequently put in sexual situations against their will.[36] Teens who are sexually abused tend to believe something is wrong with them, and they can never find wholeness and healing. Many teens victimized by sexual abuse believe they're in sin, that their sexuality is tainted, and that they've lost a great virtue they can't get back.

We must work to help teen victims to not feel trapped in their abuse and help our churches become restorative places for victims and abusers alike. If you want to understand how teen victims perceive their sexual abuse (and the responses of the church), just replace the word *abuse* with the word *sin*. On top of the fear and horror that results when someone sexually abuses them night after night, these teens suffer:

- the fear of being found out
- guilt of thinking they've brought this upon themselves, or that the sexual abuse is their fault
- anger and resentment toward their parents (both mothers and fathers)
- guilt, shame, and fear over possibly compromising and obliterating their family if this evil is discovered
- being different from their peers
- sadness about the consequences that will befall the perpetrators if or when the abuse is discovered (because while these teens hate what's being done, they may still have some loyalty toward, care for, and dependence on their abuser)

- fear of suffering retaliatory actions from other family members or even the abusers if it's discovered the abuse victims disclosed.

- fear of being condemned, shamed, confirmed worthless, and hopelessly abandoned by the church.

The frequent inability of sexually abused teens to trust adults and the church becomes a problem that seems insurmountable. This is often why the problem is kept secret.

## 1.4A INCEST

This term is commonly used for sexual relationships between closely related or immediate family members, such as parents and children, siblings and siblings, aunt or uncles and nieces or nephews; grandparents and grandchildren, and so on. Many times when the word *incest* is used it falls into the context of illegal marriage where two consenting adults in the same family are engaged in sexual relations. Incestuous relationships may also be same-sex sexual relationships between family members. Incest can also broadly include sexual relationships in blended families between stepparents and their stepchildren or between stepsiblings.

In terms of sexual abuse, between 30 percent and 40 percent of the cases of sexual victimization of teenagers and children happen in the context of family.[37] This form of incest is the sexual violation or exploitation of a minor by a familial adult caregiver (parent, grandparent, aunt, uncle, etc.). It also includes repeated, coercive sexual engagements between siblings, even if they are a few years apart in age. Many times victims are threatened to not tell anyone. The perpetrators often cover this by presenting it as a special secret between the perpetrators and the victims. Most incestuous sexual abuse starts when the victims are small children, and it's repeated throughout the victims' lives—often ending when the victims move out of their houses or the abuse is discovered. Many children and early-teen victims are led by their abusers to believe their sexual acts are normal. Later, as the teens become more knowledgeable, the abusers may threaten and manipulate them to feel responsible for the sexual encounters. Abusers may tell their teen victims they'll both go to prison if the abuse is discovered. Fear is often what keeps victims in abusive situations.

Victims of incestuous sexual abuse often harbor anger and resentment toward other family members, especially toward other adult caregivers. The victims feel trapped and believe that other parents, caregivers, or family members should see some evidence of the abuse (e.g., the abuser entering or exiting their bedrooms) and rescue and protect them. The seeming inattentiveness, lack of concern, or disinterest on the part of the other caregiver fuels a lack of trust and resentment for all adults. Many times nonabusive parents may have some suspicion of the abuse but are too afraid to confront their abusive spouses because of dependence on them for financial support and shelter, fear the abusive spouse will retaliate, or because they were abused as children and are afraid they may face the abuse again. This can create tension in the home that's often misread or blamed on teen's rebellious angst.

## 1.4B SEXUAL MISCONDUCT WITH A MINOR

*Sexual misconduct* is the term usually used for the sexual abuse of a minor by someone other than a family member. The perpetrators are usually people the teenagers know and trust and/or are in positions of authority over them (i.e., teachers, coaches, family friends, medical professionals, counselors, pastors and priests, youth workers, etc.). Those guilty of sexual misconduct engage in sexual contact with teens even if the teens consent. Again, each state regulates its own age parameters for sexual misconduct. Many states agree that sexual contact between an adult (18 and older) and a minor (under 18) is misconduct. It's also generally agreed that minors with a 60-month age difference between them and their victims can also be charged with sexual misconduct.

Because this is a delicate situation and open to various interpretations, many churches have policies regarding dating between staff of any age and youth. For instance, if a 19-year-old worship band member is dating a 17-year-old, and they become sexually active, the state can technically charge the 19-year-old with sexual misconduct because he holds a position in a ministry charged with the safety and care of minors. Normally if the same situation didn't involve a 19-year-old in a position of authority, the state wouldn't waste the time to prosecute unless a parent of the minor pressed charges. Given this scenario, the charge would be statutory rape.

Many cases of sexual misconduct go unreported because the victims fear being found out, or because they're in consensual sexual relationships with the offenders. Therefore, if a minor is in a consensual relationship, it may never be discovered by the authorities. The state of Wisconsin discovered that teen males father only 29 percent of babies born to teen mothers, while 71 percent are sired by adult males over 20 years old. In 20 percent of the cases, the fathers are at least six years older than the mothers.[38] It would be foolish to think this behavior is only confined to one state.

Many churches have faced allegations their youth pastors or youth workers were involved in sexual misconduct. Often when the public finds out about accusations, a media frenzy ensues, causing the churches to enter damage-control mode. Unfortunately, churches become consumed with protecting their reputations, leaving the victims and their abusers without the quality of care and attention needed for their restoration and redemption.

Like all sexual-abuse situations, sexual misconduct ranges from being a gross misdemeanor to a felony charge. The charge is often regulated by age difference and degree of sexual contact between the perpetrator and the victim. Many states also have first- and second-degree misconduct statutes. In most cases a second-degree misconduct charge involves any sexual contact short of vaginal or anal penetration and/or sometimes oral-genital contact. A conviction of sexual misconduct can send accused youth workers to prison and force them to register as sex offenders. (In Section 3 of this book we'll talk about how to debrief and handle the fall of a church leader.)

## 1.4C DATE RAPE

Date rape, also called acquaintance rape, is the most common form of rape. It's usually forced or coerced sexual contact between friends, dating partners, or acquaintances. Most victims of date rape know the offender. Date rape isn't limited to sexual intercourse but involves any unwanted sexual contact. The Centers for Disease Control reported that 60.4 percent of female victims and 69.2 percent of male victims were raped before the age of 18. (25.5 percent of female victims were first raped before age 12, and 34.9 percent were first raped between the ages of 12 and 17; 41 percent of male victims were first raped before age 12, and 27.9 percent were first raped between the ages of 12 and 17.) Both genders said the perpetrators were friends, family members, acquaintances, or intimate partners.[39]

In many cases with date rape, alcohol and other drugs are a factor. Alcohol and recreational drugs act as a depressant on the central nervous system. This may not seem to be the case at first because most people who become buzzed claim to be more energized and less inhibited. The reason for this is that the substance begins to depress the judgment, reasoning, and memory centers of the brain. The victim's normal inhibitions and instinctive safety assessments are dulled, giving the person a free and energized feeling. As more alcohol or drugs are consumed, judgment regarding sexual consent and contact is clouded. In addition, memory can be impaired, and a victim may black out—which makes teenagers vulnerable targets. Alcohol is still the drug of choice used by perpetrators on their victims. And because alcohol is a legal substance, it's easy to obtain.

Perpetrators sometimes use date-rape drugs on unsuspecting victims. These drugs are designed to incapacitate victims to the point where there is little or no resistance, making it easier to engage in nonconsensual sexual contact. The Drug-Induced Rape Prevention and Punishment Act of 1996 provides harsher penalties if the convicted perpetrator used a drug to sexually abuse a victim, adding up to 20 years to a sentence.[40] The most common date rape drugs are:

- Rohypnol (aka "roofies" or "rib"). This is the most common date rape drug because it can be obtained through Mexican pharmacies. An olive-green oblong pill, rohypnol is primarily used for insomnia and as a pre-anesthetic medication. As a date-rape drug it's usually crushed and slipped into a drink or mixed into food, inducing "anterograde amnesia," a condition that causes the victim to forget events that occurred while under the influence of the drug. The makers of this drug are beginning to put a dye in the drug, which when mixed in any liquid becomes activated to change the color of the drink. Other symptoms of rohypnol include feeling drunk, difficulty with motor skills, temporary loss of consciousness, slurred speech, stomach problems and nausea, and blurred vision and confusion.

- Gamma-hydroxybutyrate (GHB; also called "blue nitro" or "cherry meth"). This is an illegal substance in the United States, banned in the 1990s when it was used as a performance additive and muscle-growth stimulant for body builders. It's currently manufactured in street labs and distributed as a light-colored powder or in liquid concentrate in small hotel shampoo bottles. In liquid form the drug is odorless, tasteless, and undetectable when mixed in a drink. The powder form can have a slightly salty taste, so the most popular form of date-rape use is the liquid form. One capful of the drug usually takes effect in 15 to 30 minutes and can last from three to six hours. GHB is an anesthetic that alters the levels and transmission of dopamine in the brain. Dopamine is responsible for keeping a person alert and conscious. GHB causes the victim to lose inhibitions, relaxes muscles (yielding low motor skills), causes euphoria and hallucinations, and enhances sensuality, affection, sexual playfulness, and sexual experience. Victims often believe their sexual experiences were hallucinations or—in most cases—they may not recall the incidents at all. The euphoria created by the drug, along with the victims' inability to stay cognitively aware, makes victims unable to give consent or refuse the sexual advances of the abusers. In addition, the loss of motor skills makes victims unable to fight off the perpetrator's advances. Other effects can include dizziness, nausea, seizures, tremors, sweating, and vomiting. The drug is difficult to regulate, and the victims can easily overdose, causing coma and death.

- Ketamine (street name is "Special K"). A clear liquid or white powderlike drug primarily used as an animal tranquilizer. Like the other date-rape drugs, it can be slipped into drinks or added to smokeable materials. A victim under the influence of this drug can experience paralysis along with an effect known as "K-hole"—an out-of-body experience. The victim may be aware of being sexually abused and may come in and out of memory recall. The drug can cause delirium, amnesia, and long-term cognitive and memory problems. Other effects include dreamlike and out-of-control feelings, problems breathing, numbness, convulsions, distorted sensory perceptions, loss of coordination, and aggressive or violent behaviors.

## 1.4D SIGNS AND SYMPTOMS OF SEXUAL ABUSE

Some signs and symptoms that teens may be sexually abused include:

**Withdrawing or isolating themselves.**

**Fearing adults of a specific gender, including pulling away or avoiding them.**

**Changes in eating patterns—either a loss of appetite or sudden weight increase due to binging or overeating.**

**Changes in hygiene—failure to shower or groom, not brushing teeth, bad body odor, etc.** The victims often believe that if they're repulsive, the abuse will stop.

**Medical problems such as pain during urination, genital itching, pain and/or bleeding from abusive penetration, problems with bowel control, or the presence of venereal diseases.**

Verbal cues such as inappropriate or derogatory remarks about the perpetrators, avoiding talking at all about the perpetrators, or explicit sexual comments or conversations. Their conversation may display knowledge of sexual engagement that reveals their level of sexual experience or attempts to normalize it.

An unusual anxiety about disrobing. They may avoid any activity that requires it (e.g., sports, travel, retreats, overnights, etc.).

Hypersensitivity to criticism or worry about not pleasing authority figures.

Inability to concentrate, which can also result in poor school performance and a drop in grades.

Pronounced fear—the victims may always be "looking over their shoulders" or fearful something bad will happen.

Pronounced anxiety about going to bed at night. Many abusers often come into their victims' bedrooms late at night and wake their victims who may have fallen asleep earlier, thinking they may have escaped a night of sexual attack.

The latter may also lead to changes in sleep patterns, night-terror disorder or nightmares, and fatigue.

Other emotional or behavioral issues such as running away, self-mutilation (e.g., cutting, burning, piercing, etc.), substance use and abuse, the onset of eating disorders, night-terror disorder, depression, and suicide ideation and attempts.

Signs and symptoms that teens are victims of date-rape drugs are:

- Feeling drunk without having any drinks or drinking very little.
- Dizziness, woozy feeling, lack of controlled motor skills.
- Waking up and not remembering anything after eating or drinking (i.e., after ingesting the drug).
- Telltale signs of sexual misconduct, such as vaginal or anal pain, clothing removed, missing, or torn, etc., or a suspicion, feeling, or sense of having been sexually violated.
- Having no memory of a certain period of time.
- Any number of the symptoms mentioned under the descriptions of the date-rape drugs.

## 1.4E EFFECTS ON ABUSED MALES

The church, along with most of Western culture, is very naive to the reality, frequency, and impact of male sexual victimization. I conducted an intensive online search and couldn't find a Christian recovery program for male victims of sexual abuse. There are very few Christian resources that address this issue at all.

So much of our Western, preconceived notions about masculinity and male sexuality venerate a man for being sexually virile and "ready" anytime, anywhere, and almost any way sex is presented. When churches tell teenage guys that "all men have a sexual thought every four seconds" or "every sexual thought is lust and should be taken captive because lust is every man's battle" in the hopes of curing lust, churches unwittingly teach teenage guys they're sexual machines. Not only that, but these kinds of distorted statements actually have an inverse and negative effect on young men. They lead guys to believe that if they don't have a lust problem, aren't continuously thinking about sex, or don't desire sex all the time, then they aren't men. Yet these kinds of statements also communicate that if you do have sexual urges, desires, or feelings then you are in sin. So either way, teens formulating masculine identity are trapped by guilt.[41]

These ideations of masculinity, virility, and strength predispose us to think teenage males should never or could never be victims of sexual abuse. As such, teenage guys and adult men who've been victimized sexually rarely report because of the shame that accompanies being abused. Yet consider this:

- The U.S. Department of Health and Human Services, Centers for Disease Control, estimates that nearly one of every six male adolescents is a victim of sexual abuse.[42] These are often silent victims. Count the number of guys in your youth ministry, the sphere of your youth ministry, or obtain a number of teenage guys in your community or represented in your local high schools, then divide it by six. The number may stagger you. Male sexual abuse is common and grossly underreported, meaning many guys live with the trauma of being abused.

- Another study conducted by the Centers for Disease Control and Kaiser Permanente HMO on their members revealed that 16 percent of males were sexually abused by age 18.[43]

- The National Institute for Justice and the Centers for Disease Control reported that one in 33 American men has fallen victim to an attempted or completed rape in his lifetime. That's an estimated 2.78 million men in the U.S. having been victims of sexual assault or rape. In addition, 71 percent of male victims were first raped before they turned 18; 16.6 percent were 18 to 24 years old, and 12.3 percent were 25 or older.[44]

- 18 percent of male university students in a 1996 study reported being sexually abused before age 16.[45]

- 22 percent of sixth through eighth-grade boys surveyed in Toronto, Canada, reported being victims of sexual abuse within six weeks prior to the survey.[46] Additionally, in a 1994 Ontario study of 21,426 teenage guys, 14 percent reported parental and 18 percent nonparental sexual abuse. Canadian estimates have shown there are close to five million male victims of sexual abuse, yielding a 1 in 4 ratio of guys under age 18 who are sexually abused.[47]

We live under a cultural expectation that men are aggressive and in control. Because of this, many believe that guys cannot be sexually abused. Many believe that teenage guys can't be raped because they can fight back. They also have the notion that only weak or gay teenage guys are sexually abused. But sexual abuse, particularly a forced sexual encounter, is an act of aggression, anger, and dominance. The victims are caught off guard, over-powered, and assaulted, often under the threat of being killed. It's well known that perpetrators who rape women see them as objects to exercise aggression and dominance over. The rape is less about sexual gratification than the brutal show of aggressive force and control. But the conquest of doing the same to a male is an even greater act of dominance and control. Males who sexually assault males aren't often gay; they're abusive.

Teenage guys who are sexually abused by family members are put in subordinate positions where their well-being is continuously threatened. The sexual abuse of a male in a familial context is an act of constant domination and aggression. And the threat of others finding out about the sexual encounter is so shaming that it becomes the tool that frees the perpetrators to come back for more. Some experts say the need among male assault victims to suppress others' knowing about the assault is so powerful and pervasive that criminals such as burglars and robbers sometimes sexaully assault their male victims as a sideline solely to prevent them from going to the police.[48] Having to disclose the sexual violence along with the shaming stigma of being less of a man is greater than any other loss the victims experienced. It therefore becomes easier to see how family members, friends, or acquaintances can repeatedly keep men in sexually victimized roles. For men, to be victims of sexual abuse carries the trauma of being physically and emotionally violated along with the feeling their masculinity has been destroyed. Many male victims live silently believing they're no longer real men.

Many guys who have been sexually abused attempt to correct their shattered gender identity and loss of esteem by being overly manly. They take issue with being touched or shown affection (most likely because they still have fears regarding that). They adopt macho stereotypes, become more aggressive, and play out warrior archetypal tendencies. They seem emotionally cold and distant because emotion is a show of weakness. If abused by women, they may view women in general with disdain, objectify them, or treat them as lower-class people; if abused by men, they may be very verbal and militant about their disgust for gays, engage in gay-bashing, berate weaker or effeminate men, and avoid any stereotypical behavior that may associate them with homosexuality or femininity.

Teenage guys can be raped by women or men. The belief that males are raped only by other men in prisons is faulty. So is the belief that male sexual abuse is always perpetrated by males. Many teenage guys are forced, manipulated, or threatened by older women to enter sexual relationships with them. Familial sexual abuse between a mother and son or a relationship initiated by an older sister with a brother is very real. Outside the family boys have been forced to perform sexual acts with their girlfriends' mothers for fear of being banned from their girlfriends; female teachers have threatened to fail male students, have them cut from sports teams, or jeopardize scholarships if they didn't perform sexual favors.

Many in our society view this as an opportunity to champion the virile male sex-machine mentality and encourage guys to go for it. They see this as a sexual rite of passage into experienced sexual manhood. Some may even comment that they wish it had happened to them (again reinforcing the notion a man is measured by his sexual bravado). But sex is more than a physiological act. Male sexual abuse victims report having the same feelings, fears, guilt, shame, and trauma as female sexual abuse victims.

Early in my youth ministry, a woman in my church asked me to meet with her 19-year-old son. He was living at home, difficult to control, continually in trouble with the law, and struggling with substance abuse. He had an obvious disdain for church but still agreed to meet with me.

In the course of our conversation he disclosed that his mother's best friend had made sexual advances toward him when he was 13 years old, and he "lost his virginity" with her. According to him, he still felt bad and believed he was responsible for what happened. He also lived with the threat that if his mother found out she'd lose her best friend. He presented the whole experience to me in a positive light, claiming it to be manly. He liked the fact that he was getting some action every week, and that an older woman was interested in him. Yet he couldn't understand what drove his behaviors and addictions. He'd never consider bringing charges against the woman because in his mind that would assault his masculinity more than the act of sexual abuse he experienced.

If male sex victims have erections and/or experience ejaculation during sexual assaults, it doesn't mean they enjoyed the assaults or wanted them. Males are easily stimulated by touch. They can have erections even under the pressure of fear and trauma, even if they're drugged or under the influence of alcohol, even if they're repulsed by the actions they're engaging in, etc. An erection is not an act of volition; it's the result of vasocongestion (i.e., increased blood flow), and ejaculation is an involuntary physiological response to genital stimulation. Many abusers attempt to bring their male victims to ejaculation because it makes them feel they've succeeded in controlling and dominating their victims. Guys who're sexually abused repeatedly may realize that ejaculation can put a quick end to the process, so they may submit, allowing themselves to reach ejaculation faster. Their ultimate goal, like women who are repeatedly sexually abused, is to just get the abuse over with fast.

Guys who experience sexual abuse by males are not, nor will they become, gay men. Similarly, many men who sexually assault teenage guys are not necessarily gay, but rather want to dominate them, as mentioned previously. Note: Many gay teenage guys become victims of gay date rape or are abused by gay adults. Some gay teenagers are sexually abused repeatedly by straight male family members or friends as acts of anti-gay aggression. This kind of abuse is often accompanied by verbal and physical abuse. And just because a teenage guy is gay doesn't mean he enjoys the forced sexual encounter any more than a straight teen guy enjoys the abuse of an older woman. Homophobia and fear of being considered gay is a real motivation that keeps straight male teenage victims from reporting sexual abuse.

Many believe that gay teenage guys are asking to be sexually abused. Similarly, many believe girls who're sexually abused are provoking the actions against them. Both of these are terrible misconceptions—no one is "asking for" or deserves abuse.

Guys more than girls fear the public exposure of their victimization. It assaults their gender identity, as well as their notions of strength, control, and sexual orientation. Further, the church finding out adds the fear of being labeled a sexual sinner (which they're already feeling). Remember Chris, the student who admitted a babysitter abused him? He experienced the culmination of all those fears. He felt like he wasn't a man any longer, nor was he pure, nor was he qualified to serve in ministry...and the list goes on.

Many abused teenage boys suffer humiliation and retaliatory assaults from family members and friends once the incident is exposed. Comments such as, "Why didn't you just fight back?" or, "If I was in that situation, I would've kicked his @#% before I let him do that to me!" are often made and erode an already destroyed esteem and identity of the male victims.

For many boys the abuse starts early in their childhoods and then consistently carries into their teenage years. They come into even greater confusion when their bodies change, and they experience their first ejaculation during abusive encounters. The confusion of the pleasurable feeling juxtaposed against the ongoing trauma of the experience creates confusion and shame.

## 1.5 SELF-ABUSE

Self-abuse isn't usually included in the standard list of abuse, but this contemporary issue is on the rise and very prevalent in the scope of youth ministry. Teenage guys and teenage girls self-abuse and self-mutilate.

Let's start with a point of clarification: In the earlier history of the church, the term *self-abuse* referred to the act of masturbation. The church held to views that this behavior was an act of personal violation and heinous abuse. There is still some residual of that belief. We're not talking about masturbation at all when referring to self-abuse. Self-abuse, self-harm, deliberate self-harm, para-suicidal behavior, or nonsuicidal self-injury are interchangeable terms used among professionals to describe acts of pain and destruction inflicted upon an individual by herself. Self-abuse can also include self-deprecation, self-starvation, drug and alcohol abuse, risky and harmful behaviors such as starting fights, reckless driving, having unprotected sex with strangers, etc. Self-harm often becomes the symptom of some underlying, greater issue or disorder. Teens who self-abuse are not attempting to severely injure themselves, nor are they attempting suicide. There are many reasons why teenagers may self-abuse:

- Some report that the external physical pain diverts their attention or becomes a relief to the internal pain and turmoil they are experiencing. The frequent infliction of pain also creates an endorphin rush that becomes the body's natural way of reducing physical stress. Many times self-harm reduces the ideation of suicide.

- Some experience a phenomenon called alexithymia, or an inability to find any words to express their emotions. Self-harm becomes the outward expression for the emotional storm that holds the individuals captive.

- Some report that self-abuse makes them feel alive or real. This may be an example of the opposite of alexithymia, in that the patient feels nothing—a form of athymia. Therefor the infliction of pain on themselves reminds them they do in fact have feelings and are alive.

- Some use this as a form of self-punishment. They have such a hatred and anger for themselves that they desire to self-injure. Many self-abusing teens are often experiencing abuse (physical, verbal, but mostly sexual) from others. They blame themselves for the abuse and then follow similar patterns by abusing themselves.

- Some cause injury to themselves as desperate acts or cries for help. While most self-abusers don't want to be discovered, some hope a medical professional, counselor, youth worker, or caregiver will ask them about their injury. This becomes the opportunity for others to step into their silent pain.

## 1.5A FORMS OF SELF-MUTILATION

**Cutting.** This is the most common form. Many youth workers have seen a rise in this form of self-abuse. While it seems girls are more frequently cutters, this form of abuse is also prevalent with males. Teens who cut use any sharp objects available, including razor blades, knives, shards of glass, metal, and even their fingernails. This form of abuse can range from scraping the skin raw to deep lacerations. Most cutters inflict pain on their arms, upper legs and thighs, and even torsos. These are places that can be concealed, which is why wearing clothing inappropriate for warmer weather (long-sleeved shirts, long pants, etc.) may be symptomatic of self-abuse.

**Branding or burning.** In this case a hot iron, heated piece of metal, soldering iron, or any object that can get hot enough to burn skin is used. The hot object is then applied to arms, legs, or torso leaving a burn wound. Sometimes this wound will keloid, or become a thick red or pink raised scar from overgrowth of tissue. Infection can often set in, causing more pain and the need of immediate medical attention. Branding is often used as an underground form of body modification. When teens are doing this to themselves, most always it's a form of self-abuse and not a fashion statement.

**Self-flagellation.** This form of abuse involves beating oneself with straps, whips, chains, bats, hammers, pipes, etc. These objects can often leave marks, bruises, broken or fractured bones, concussions, and a host of other infirmities. Variations on this form of self-abuse involve banging one's head against immovable objects such as walls or tables, punching walls or other objects that won't give, or slamming oneself into walls. These actions obviously can render victims dizzy, disoriented, delirious, or even unconscious.

**Piercing or tattooing.** This is a common, culturally accepted form of body art or augmentation. Many teens get piercings or tattoos as rites of passage into adulthood. Both are pain-inducing but can be endured to make fashion statements. The line of fashion is crossed to self-abuse when teens begin to pierce or tattoo themselves. Like the other forms of self-abuse, the pain inflicted numbs the teens to the emotional pain within. Most piercings are done through soft tissue such as earlobes, nipples, etc. The pain is often increased when cartilage or other types of tissue are pierced (between fingers and toes, laterally on arms, legs, torso and neck, etc.).

**Trichotillomania.** This is an impulse disorder in which teens pull out their own hair. Most often the disorder begins at the onset of early adolescence and is triggered by some life trauma such as sexual abuse. Teens experiencing trichotilliomania tend to pull out bits of hair to small tresses, leaving bald patches and sores all over their heads. If the pulling is severe enough, they can pull away patches of skin or uproot hair, leaving permanent bald spots. The result of this self-abusive behavior leads to embarrassment, loss of self-esteem, and ridicule from friends and family. Abusers cannot conceal this form of abuse for long, but as a temporary measure teens may wear hats or keep their heads covered all the time. In some cases, medications can be administered to help curb the impulse to harm oneself.

**Dermatillomania.** Like the latter, this form of self-abusive behavior involves picking, pulling, and breaking the skin. It's often played out by keeping an old wound opened by scraping or picking it. The abuser may also resort to biting in order to inflict the wound.

## 1.5B SYMPTOMS OF SELF-ABUSE
**Physical wounds, cuts, bruises, bite marks, welts, etc.** One may first assume that teens are being physically abused by others. They evidence the same symptoms.

**Inappropriate seasonal clothing or bizarre clothing to hide wounds.** A number of wristbands that never come off, or anything else that may conceal marks. One girl came into a youth group with various scarves and colored cloth tied all up and down her arm, presenting as a fashion statement what was in reality the concealment of the marks of her self-abuse.

**Objects such as bats, chains, broken glass, razor blades, soldering irons, etc., in their bedrooms.**

**Isolating oneself or spending long periods of time alone in bedrooms or bathrooms.**

**Self-abasing talk.** These teens may not take compliments well and tend to put themselves down or become very angry when they feel they've failed in any way.

**Paralleled signs and symptoms of the other forms listed here.** Remember that self-abuse is often a secondary behavior to some experienced trauma or emotional issue going on with teens.

## 1.6 PROFILE OF ABUSERS

- They come from all socioeconomic levels, both genders, all ethnicities and races, and can vary in age.

- They have poor self-esteem or are very insecure. This is evidenced by a need to control their surroundings and the people in their spheres of influence. The opposite may also be seen; an abuser may have a grandiose view of self. This form of dictatorial arrogance often demonstrates his disregard for everyone.

Thus many people can feel abused in the form of disrespected, berated or belittled, devalued, and the list goes on.

- They're manipulative, threatening, and controlling.

- Abusers often become jealous and spiteful toward anyone in close relationship with their teen victims, especially boyfriends or girlfriends.

- They have poor impulse control, are easily provoked, don't think about what they're saying or doing, nor consider the consequences of their behaviors.

- They minimize the seriousness of the abuse, tend to see the abuse as a normal response of discipline, and tend to blame the problem on their victims. They may also have elaborate, fabricated stories about the reason the teens made allegations or are showing physical signs of abuse.

- They are bossy, authoritarian, and demanding.

- They may have drug and/or alcohol problems.

- Many times they manipulate their victims by endearing behavior (i.e., they are charming, loving, giving, etc.).

## 1.7 MANDATED REPORTING

In 1989 the United Nations adopted the Convention on the Rights of a Child. This 54-article instrument was entered into force in January of 2002 and became the first legally binding international document protecting the rights, freedoms, needs, care, and survival of all children under the age of 18 worldwide. Among those articles were protection rights that include protection from abuse, neglect, cruelty, exploitation, and even ensuring special protection during times of war and from criminal justice systems. Countries that signed the Convention agreed to enact laws that ensure the safety of children from abuse. Many of these countries have mandated reporting laws for professionals and volunteers who work with minors. Like the United States, many of these countries vary on their definition of who a minor is, who is required to report, what constitutes abuse, etc. While 192 countries of the U.N. General Assembly signed the document, two did not: The United States and Somalia. Yet the United States has rights that protect its children, including child-abuse mandated reporting laws.

All 50 U.S. states have mandated reporting laws with regard to child abuse and neglect. Specifications on who is mandated to report vary from state to state. Most states include any person who works with or has consistent contact with minors. This would include teachers, doctors, counselors, people who work in youth organizations, etc. Some states require volunteer workers to report as well, while other states may not mandate volunteers to report. As a point of clarification, because a certain group isn't mandated to report doesn't mean they can't or shouldn't report if they see or are suspicious of abuse. Many states mandate church employees, ordained or not, to report. Some states, however, allow clergy to be exempt from reporting if they come into the knowledge of the abuse in a confessional or in some form of penitential communication disclaimer. For example, if an adult confesses abuse of a teenager to a youth pastor in one of these states, the youth pastor may honor confidentiality and provide sanctuary to the adult while seeking to bring correction to the situation. However, mandatory reporting laws in that same state could require the youth pastor to report if he has witnessed abuse, hears the minor disclose the abuse, or hears of the abuse in a nonpenitential setting prior to the confession.

Mandatory reporting laws also get complex when it comes to volunteers. While some states don't require volunteers to report, they do require other professionals to report if they are volunteering. That means that school teachers who serve at churches never cease to be mandatory reporters, even in their roles as church volunteers. Some states require that all agents of organizations that work with minors, including volunteers, are mandated to report abuse and suspicion of abuse. To find out your state's reporting requirements, go to The Child Welfare Information Gateway at www.childwelfare.gov/systemwide/laws_policies/state/.

It's important a church's policies and practices be aligned with the state's requirements. It's unethical to do anything apart from mandated reporting laws. I know of some churches that require volunteers to tell youth pastors when they suspect abuse. The youth pastors must bring this concern to senior pastors and church boards for reviews and rulings. While it's necessary for church leadership to be informed and involved, volunteers who are considered mandatory reporters cannot wait for committees' rulings on whether they should take the information to child protective agencies. If the state requires an individual to report, the policies of the church should never interfere with that. Some states also require mandatory reporters to orally report within 24 hours of obtaining their knowledge of the abuse and 48 hours if a written report is required. The state won't consider the policies of the church if it decides to bring legal action against the mandated reporter. Many states impose strict fines and prison sentences against mandated reporters who fail to report.

Child protective agencies in every state have anonymous reporting venues. People can call the National Child Abuse Hotline (1-800-4-A-CHILD) and report without giving their names. It's a misconception that children will be immediately removed from homes because of reports, or that a person has the right to know who reported.[49]

If you're a mandated reporter according to your state's statutes, you're required to give your name and phone number. This information will be kept confidential, but documented to protect you by showing that you reported as required.

Most states say that mandated reporters are required to report when they're presented with reasonable cause to believe that a minor is being abused or neglected. This gives the mandated reporter some latitude in exercising judgment in determining this (e.g., Was the teen joking? Exaggerating? Lying? etc.). Reasonable cause to suspect child abuse or maltreatment means that, based on your observations, training, and experience, you believe that a child (a minor) has been harmed or placed in imminent danger of harm.[50] Some states require that mandatory reporters complete state-approved

training courses to help determine things such as reasonable cause. Many churches are unaware these courses exist.

When youth workers contact child protective services, officials there may ask for the following information:

- The nature of the harm or the specific incidents that precipitated the report.

- Identities of the accused and their relationships to the abused.

- Witnesses to the incident and how they may be contacted.

- Details of any physical evidence you may have observed. This would include cuts, bruises, etc.; their specific location, etc.

- If the accused have access to or are currently with the victim(s).

- Assessment of the abused teen's present condition: Does the teen need medical attention? Is the teen presently staying in the home? With friends? Has the teen run away? Describe the teen's disposition, etc.

- Exact details of what the teen said that prompted your call.

- You'll have the opportunity to give your personal assessment of the situation. You may want to share pertinent information about the teen (e.g., if she is attention-seeking or histrionic) Your responsibility is to share your observations and opinions. The agency will make the assessment and devise a plan of action if necessary.

# Understanding How Theology Informs the Issue of Teenage Abuse

## | Section 2 |

## 2.1 THEOLOGY THAT INFORMS THE ISSUES RELATED TO ABUSE

### 2.1A IDENTITY IN CHRIST

It's rare that teens who are physically or sexually abused are not also verbally abused. Verbal abuse has a devastating psychological effect on teenagers. Adolescence is when we formulate our identities, beginning with gender identities and then our personal identities. Abuse always impacts identity formation. Verbally abused teens internalize messages they're worthless and unwanted. When teens are also sexually abused, they struggle further to discover their identities and the physical changes that are happening to their bodies.

The church must step in and show victims how God sees them, thinks of them, and what God says about them from the Bible. A good starting place is Philippians 1:6: "Being confident of this, that he who began a good work in you will carry it on to completion until the day of Christ Jesus." Abused teens need to know that God designed them well! Here are some other truths that can help teens formulate their identities in Christ:

- You're God's Child (John 1:12; Romans 8:14-15; Galatians 3:26; 1 John 3:1-2)

- You're Christ's Friend (John 15:15)

- You're Chosen and Beloved of God (John 15:16; Colossians 3:12)

- You're an Heir with Christ (Romans 8:17; Galatians 4:6-7)

- You're a New Creation (2 Corinthians 5:17)

- You're Holy and Righteous (Ephesians 4:24)

- You're Free from Condemnation (Romans 8:1)

- You're Made Complete in Christ (Colossians 2:10)

- You're Approved by God (2 Timothy 2:15)

- You're Born of God and the Devil Can't Touch You (1 John 5:18)

- You're a Member of Christ's Body (1 Corinthians 12:27; Ephesians 5:30)

- You're a Citizen of Heaven (Ephesians 2:19; Philippians 3:20)

## 2.1B RECONCILIATION AND REDEMPTION

When dealing with teens and families who've experienced abuse, it's important we have a clear theological view of reconciliation (meaning God makes things right) and redemption (meaning God makes things better than they were before). God has given us a ministry of reconciliation (2 Corinthians 5:11-21), and we're reminded old things pass away and all things are made new. This is the powerful hope we live in.

## 2.1C DISCIPLINE IN PROVERBS

Youth workers may be called upon to help parents discern the difference between punishment, discipline, and abuse. Many Christian parents don't know the difference and struggle to discern how God disciplines his children. The starting point in discerning and forming a theological view on discipline can be found in Proverbs. There are four passages in the book of Proverbs that give wise instruction on discipline:

- Proverbs 13:24—"Those who spare the rod hates their children, but those who love them are careful to discipline them."
- Proverbs 22:15—"Folly is bound up in the heart of a child, but the rod of discipline will drive it far away."
- Proverbs 23:13-14—"Do not withhold discipline from children; if you punish them with the rod, they will not die. Punish them with the rod and save them from death."

Some take these verses as proof God is for corporal (physical) punishment, while others don't believe these passages should be taken literally. Both miss the point: The rod of discipline is a symbol of a long, consistent lifestyle of coaching a child. Proverbs is a book that uses a mentoring model of a wiser, older man passing wisdom down to a younger man. The point of these verses is that discipline is the very thing that will spur on children to seek wisdom all their lives and banish foolishness from their hearts. That lifelong discipline is the theme of the book of Proverbs. These passages are a challenge to the younger man to begin to invest in his own children. This is not about an occasional timeout (noncorporal) or an occasional spanking (corporal) when a child gets out of line. The fourth and probably most powerful passage is:

- Proverbs 22:6—"Train a child in the way he should go, and when he is old he will not turn from it." (NIV)

Let's break this verse down phrase by phrase in order to understand it better: "Train a child" means that as soon as children can understand, we should dedicate them to the truth. So discipline starts at the beginning of life. "In the way he should go" carries with it the idea that discipline should be applied according to the uniqueness of a child's character, development, and temperament. "And when he is old" implies discipline is important throughout life in order to move toward maturity. "He will not turn from it"—is this the payoff or guarantee? No! It means disciplined children will never escape the discipline instilled in them. It implies that the thirst for truth will be imbedded, internalized, and become part of that child's nature. If we put those meanings together it would read something like this:

"As soon as children can understand, dedicate them to truth. Train them according to the uniqueness of their character, development, and temperament. Then, all throughout their maturity, the thirst for truth will be imbedded, internalized, and become part of their nature."

## 2.1D CARING FOR ORPHANS AND WIDOWS

James 1:27 reads, "Religion that God our Father accepts as pure and faultless is this: to look after orphans and widows in their distress and to keep oneself from being polluted by the world." When an abuser is convicted or if there's enough evidence to merit an investigation, minors become wards of the state. In effect, they become orphaned. Many minors don't want abuse to be discovered because they don't want their families shattered. Teens who have younger siblings often shoulder the physical abuse to protect those young ones—and for fear they'll end up split apart and orphaned. Our churches should be ready to step in and take action in these circumstances. Families within our churches should stand up and be prepared to legally take minors in when families go through crises. The church is called to safeguard orphans. Additionally, when parents are convicted of abuse, they often leave spouses behind—in effect, widows (or widowers).

The victims and their families need the church more than ever. But churches often aren't sure how to support them and don't have a plan to bring sanctuary and healing. (I speak more of the effects of abuse on a wife and family in Section 3.3.)

## 2.2: QUESTIONS THAT DEMAND THEOLOGICAL CONSIDERATION

### 2.2A: WHY DOESN'T GOD ANSWER MY PRAYERS AND SAVE ME FROM ABUSE?

Teens who are being abused or have experienced abuse may pray fervently God will deliver them. Remember the story I told in the first section about a girl who anonymously asked the church to pray? She probably prayed continually for God to put an end to her abuse. Abused teens are in moment-by-moment hell. Their hurt, turmoil, defeat, shame, guilt, and humiliation are devastating. They pray for relief but sometimes none comes. Then they may believe that God doesn't care about them, or that their sins have disqualified their prayers. Abused teens may have many questions about prayer and why God doesn't deliver them from their abusers. This should call youth workers to have well-thought-through theologies of prayer. (Fortunately, volumes have been written on this subject.) In the end it's your responsibility to help teens navigate these issues, so start developing a personal theology of prayer.

## 2.2B WHY DOES GOD ALLOW ABUSE?

At the core of this question is an understanding of evil, pain, and suffering. It's difficult for adults (let alone teens) to wrap their minds around why God allows pain and suffering. The most important thing we must get through to abused teens is that they're not suffering because of sin in their lives. Often abused teens believe that is the reason God allows the abuse. All of the New Testament proclaims that Jesus paid for all our sins. Therefore we need to usher teens into this hope. For more on developing a theology of evil, suffering, and pain see the book on dealing with death in this series: *What Do I Do When... Teenagers Deal with Death?*

## 2.2C SHOULD A FALLEN LEADER BE RESTORED?

If church leaders (clergy, lay, or volunteer youth worker) are convicted of abusing minors, the law immediately disqualifies them from working with minors. I fully believe that convicted child abusers should not be allowed to work with minors in the church or any other context. While the abuser is disqualified from working with minors, he is never disqualified from the relentless pursuit of God's amazing grace. And the church is God's agent to bring this grace into the life of the abuser.

Ministry to the abuser doesn't stop because that individual shattered many people, and maybe even the reputation of the church. We need to remember  Christ's parable illustrating that the King comes and finds that his own rejected him. When asked, he explains that He was in prison and they did not minister to him. The church must minister and usher grace into the lives of those whom others seem to think are disqualified from grace.

But what happens when leaders are accused of inappropriate actions that are not substantiated and never lead to convictions? I've seen people removed from ministry just because of gossip, suspicion, and rumors of misconduct. Church leadership has become quick to judge at the hint of any wrongdoing. My story in the preface of this book is a clear example of the problem. Sin and failures must be dealt with using care and a deep desire to bring restoration to those who've fallen. Most often churches seek to quickly find out the facts and remove the problem—which usually means firing staff members and encouraging them to leave their churches.

The church has a responsibility to minister healing to both victims and abusers. No matter how heinous the sin, our role is to seek restoration. This is a difficult perspective to take, especially when people deceived the church and used their positions of authority to leverage power over minors. Yet the truth is inescapable: The church has been given a ministry of reconciliation.

In Galatians 6:1-4, the apostle Paul writes, "Brothers and sisters, if someone is caught in a sin, you who live by the Spirit should restore that person gently. But watch yourselves, or you also may be tempted. Carry each other's burdens, and in this way you will fulfill the law of Christ. If any of you think you are something when you are nothing, you deceive yourselves. Each of you should test your own actions. Then you can take pride in yourself, without comparing yourself to somebody else."

Seeking restoration is extremely challenging in abuse situations. It's easy for us to see the sins of others as greater than our own. When we lose the perspective that each of us is a sinner, we fall into sin as well, which renders us useless in the process of restoration. In our piety we may long for a sense of justice, desiring that the guilty parties pay for their sins, but we must remember that Jesus already paid for each person's sin with his life.

Often adults found in sexual entanglements with minors go to jail. We must be gracious, loving, and consistent to minister to them, even while they're incarcerated. Without question this is an incredibly difficult and delicate matter. But Jesus mandated us to "look after those who are in prison," caring for them just as we would care for the Savior himself (Matthew 25:34-46). The church must have an active, aggressive commitment to bring healing to fallen leaders even while they're in prison.

Not only are we commanded to love, but also we're commanded to forgive those who've hurt us greatly. Paul reminds us, "If anyone has caused grief, he has not so much grieved me as he has grieved all of you to some extent—not to put it too severely. The punishment inflicted on him by the majority is sufficient. Now instead, you ought to forgive and comfort him, so that he will not be overwhelmed by excessive sorrow. I urge you, therefore, to reaffirm your love for him" (2 Corinthians 2:5-8).

Forgiveness is the ultimate test of our love...and love is the defining mark for followers of Jesus. Love is the command Jesus left us—the church—and the true test of our character and obedience.

## 2.3 SCRIPTURE PASSAGES TO CONSIDER
Philippians 2:1-5—This passage should be the starting point regarding how teens should treat each other in a relational context.

**Matthew 5:31-48; James 1:27**—These verses give us a good picture of the kinds of actions disciples should take toward those who've been abused and those who are abusers.

**Galatians 6:1-10**—This passage instructs leaders to restore, in a gracious and loving way, and act in a way that's good to those who've fallen. The reaping and sowing in the context of the passage is regarding the law of Christ (to be loving and good). If leaders don't act in a forgiving, loving manner with every intention to restore, those leaders will reap an unforgiving, unloving destruction. (Compare this passage to Matthew 7:1-3 and Luke 6:36-38.)

**Matthew 18:1-6**—Jesus pronounces a woe on people who cause or lead minors into sin.

**James 3:1**—a sobering account for anyone who teaches.

# Practical Action to Take When Teenagers Are Victims of Albuse

## | Section 3 |

### 3.1 PLANNING AHEAD

The worst time to figure out what you should do with an abuse situation is when it's presented to you. Most youth ministries don't have a clue what to do until it's too late. If we're to minister effectively to hurting teens and families, we must have a plan. The best thing to do is be prepared *before* you're confronted with abuse. The following are some starting points:

**Know state mandates, policies, and procedures.** Make sure staffers know who to call and what's required of them.

**Make sure church staff, youth workers, volunteers, and parents know warning signs of abuse.**

**Consider posting a notice in your youth room for teens and parents that states that your ministry will be a caring, safe place.** The notice should also state that if a teen talks to anyone on your staff regarding issues of abuse, then you're mandated by state law to report those issues to the proper authorities. Such a notice may also include the phone number of an anonymous helpline teens can call to get assistance.

People who work with youth should never make blanket promises of confidentiality. If harm is being done to a youth, you may be mandated to report. Additionally, if teenagers are harming others, or if teenagers are harming themselves—these are not confidential issues. When lives are in danger, we're mandated by law to report. Under tort laws, civil action can be taken if it's proved that youth workers had prior knowledge of harm being done to teenagers and did not inform authorities.

**Train others who work with teens and children to take appropriate steps if presented with abuse situations.**

- Remain calm and listen when teens confide in you about abuse. Certain reactions will stop teens from sharing and make them feel unsafe. Avoid showing signs of disgust, challenging the validity of what the teens are saying, or giving the impression the teens may be overreacting.

- Reassure the teens they did nothing to provoke this abusive behavior. Assure them the abusers will never know of your conversation; however, that you cannot promise confidentiality because child protective services may require you to report, or you may feel the need to report to protect them. Your church leadership may also need to know the information and the steps you're required to take or plan to take.

- Before your conversation with a teen, be aware of the information child protective services may need from you. Ask clarifying questions of the teen, but avoid interrogating the teen or doing you own investigating. It should also be the policy of your church to do no investigating, but commit to notifying child protective services within 24 hours of learning of the abuse. Investigation belongs to professionals who know how to do it and what to look for.

- If the teen is in danger, he must be protected. The teen should not be unsupervised or allowed to leave, return home, etc. In addition the youth worker should immediately find two other people to be a party to protecting the teen. These people should be with you and the teen as soon as possible (it's always wise for a church to make a policy that there will be at least three adults, representative of both genders, present whenever teens are at the church). This deters a potential perpetrator from targeting you in a violent reprisal. If the danger is immediate, call 911 and notify the police. They will collaborate with other agencies to have the teen safeguarded. Do not take the teen to your home or promise he can stay with you until you've contacted the proper authorities and have clearance.

- Reassure teens of your continued support. Let them know that you'll never judge or think less of them, but will always hold them in the highest esteem and value. Encourage teens that there is hope—and that what they're doing now is an important step toward ending the abuse.

- Make the call to child protective services. The National Child Abuse Hotline is a 24-hour line: 800-4-A-CHILD (or 800-422-4453). You can also call your state's child protective services (numbers are listed by state in the resource section of this book). They can guide you through appropriate next steps if needed. Be aware that if the teen is not in immediate danger or in need of medical attention, child protective services may not respond with immediacy but will respond in a timely manner (you may never know when or how they responded, especially if your call is anonymous). Also be aware child protective services may not respond at all. They may not have enough information to take any more action. Your call will ensure the situation is on record and can be referenced should further reports become necessary. If others respond in the future regarding the safety of the same teen, a more thorough investigation will take place. Remember: Your report makes a difference because it's on file. Take into consideration also that you're emotionally invested because you know, love, and care for this teen who's hurting—that will color your perspective regarding how you think things should be handled. Encourage the teen to talk to other trusted adults, such as school counselors, teachers, coaches, or others you know are mandated reporters in the teen's life.

- Discreetly monitor the teen by asking direct questions. Let the teen know you're being supportive. If the perpetrator is a family member who attends your church, be aware this person may be constantly watching the teen. Have your conversations in public places, keep them short, be pleasant as you talk with the teen, allow others to approach you both but change the subject immediately. These measures will protect the teen and divert suspicion in the mind of a watchful perpetrator. If you usher the teen away to a private place to have a deep conversation, the abuser may grow suspicious and retaliate. Be sure to be natural and true to your personality.

**Let parents and others know your action policy if you believe a minor is being abused.** If a minor claims to be abused or if there is some suspicion of abuse, you will immediately contact child protective services to avoid any interference in the investigation should legal action need to be taken. Parents will not be notified or questioned by the church.

**Establish church policies and protocol regarding suspected abuse including confidentiality protocol, immediate and long-term action that will be taken, reporting chain of command (the fewer people in this queue, the better), appropriate protocol for staff, and rules regarding public information.**

**Network with Christian counselors and social workers to build a good referral base for families in crisis.** If you're unfamiliar with mental health professionals in your area, contact the nearest Christian university and seek referrals in your area from their psychology and counseling departments. You can also network with other area churches to find recommended mental health workers.

## 3.2 HELPING TEENS WHO SELF-ABUSE

**Confront in a gentle, loving way.** If you think teens are cutting, ask them. First verbalize your love and concern. Reassure the teens that you're not judging, repulsed by, or condemning them. Tell them what your observations are and that you believe they may be deliberately hurting themselves. Ask to see their arms or ask them how they got the wounds you do see.

**Initiate open communication with teens.** Be committed to listen and always ask open-ended questions such as, "What makes you want to hurt yourself?" Don't be quick to offer solutions, just listen.

**Make the parents or caregivers aware you know self-injury is happening (make sure you know by verifying it with the teens).** Suggest that the parents seek a counselor and give them some referrals. Ask them how you or the church can be a further help to their family. Some parents may not know what to do with the situation. Your acknowledgment of the problem makes them aware someone else is monitoring the situation.

**If you see wounds or signs of infection, or if teens are severely hurt, seek immediate medical attention.** Ask to see their injuries and how they injured themselves so you can help assess the severity of their wounds.

**Help teens learn alternative coping skills** (e.g., journaling feelings, talking through issues, physical activities like running, swimming, dance, or aerobics, finding hobbies, etc.).

**Help them build emotional support networks of at least three people they can talk with.** At least two should be adults (one should ideally be a parent).

**Clean house.** Together with a parent or trusted adult, have the teen collect all the paraphernalia she uses to self-injure. Like an addict, a self-abuser will hide the things used to inflict injury.

**Help self-abusing teens learn appropriate ways to express themselves as alternatives to self-harming.** Suggest setting up a corner in the garage where they can paint, write poetry, sing and/or dance, etc.

**Refer.** Remember that self-abuse is often a symptom of a deeper unseen issue. Also remember you're not a trained counselor, and your best course of action is to connect teens and their families to experienced Christian counselors.

## 3.3 DEALING WITH YOUTH MINISTER AND LEADER MISCONDUCT

The moral failure and misconduct of church leaders is always complex. So many people are affected by the situation: church families, staff and leadership, community leaders and authorities, teens and the youth group, parents who feel trust has been violated, and the offenders and their families (if they have them). And if that weren't complicated enough, there's the media. From my experience as a counselor and consultant—and the input of others who've gone through similar experiences—here are some tips to remember:

**Consider bringing in a consultant (such as a counselor).** This person should be a neutral party who can help the church staff and leaders think clearly and objectively. The consultant can debrief the staff, help church leadership navigate the storm, assist in crafting and editing communications, help with the overall care of the church, help establish appropriate plans of action, and troubleshoot and coach the church through the aftermath.

**Before crises ever occur, churches should build crisis response teams that can serve as "crisis central" when one hits.** This team should handle the church's response to every crisis from natural disasters to fallen staff members. The crisis response team should field all questions from the church, from the community, and from the media. This team should also oversee the actions taken by the church, including the restoration of the victim and the victim's family and the care of the fallen leader and his family. The team should be pre-trained and ready to respond as needed. This team should include these members:

- A staff member who will coach the other staff as to what to say and not say, the facts they should know, updating them on proceedings, and caring for their hurts. The initial care for staff may best be done by an outside consultant, counselor, or spiritual director. This response team member becomes the representative of the staff, protecting the staff from being drawn into the fire. It also eliminates the "he said, she said" games between staff and the church.

- Someone who'll field all communications from and to the media. It's best to say as little as possible and engage the community directly.

- Someone who'll oversee the care and counseling for those in your church apart from the victim and victim's family and the offender and offender's family.

- Someone who'll either serve as the church's legal counsel or work closely with legal counsel. When child abuse charges or sexual misconduct charges are filed, legal counsel must be obtained to keep parties who are connected to the case from saying or doing anything that would jeopardize an investigation.

- Someone who'll work directly with the victim and her family through recovery, restoration, and wholeness. This response team member doesn't do the counseling but becomes the person who makes sure the family is being cared for.

- Another person who'll do the same for the offender and his family. If the offender is married and has children, they often suffer most. Churches forget that if they fire leaders, or if leaders are sent to prison, those leaders' families don't suffer just the humiliation and hurt of the situation, they also may suffer the loss of income, incur huge legal fees, undergo the pain of possibly moving, and experience the loss of privacy because of the actions of the media and community, among other unforeseen things. The response people who work with the victim and the offender and their families should be aware they could be subpoenaed to testify in court if they learn of information. Therefore they must be trained to stay on the task of caring for the needs of the families and not being the sounding boards for details and opinions offered by the parties they serve. All must remain neutral, and so, guard their comments, conversations, and information. It's important the response people be agents of care and mobilize resources from those involved.

## 3.3A WARNING SIGNS OF A YOUTH MINISTER'S MISCONDUCT
**If a youth worker's only circle of friends consists of the teenagers to whom she ministers, a warning light should go off.** Youth workers need to have friends their age and older. If your church

doesn't have people in the same age range as your youth worker (some churches are void of early and mid-twentysomethings), then the youth worker should be encouraged to attend a Bible study or young adult ministry at another church. Youth workers can also seek to build friendships with area youth workers, those in accountability networks, and students at local Christian universities or seminaries.

**If youth workers have deep desires to be liked, needed, and accepted by teens, they're likely to fall.** Most often there are other serious compromises that occur before any sexual misappropriation, such as having long, intimate talks that influence teens to violate parental curfews, drinking with minors, smoking, watching porn, etc. The need for acceptance or to be liked becomes a slippery slope that can lead to severe consequences.

**Make sure all people who work with minors undergo background checks.** This is a safeguard, but it doesn't ensure incidents never take place. Background checks only reveal convictions of sexual misconduct or outstanding warrants. In addition to background checks, make sure those who work with minors have one or two references who could vouch for their character. This should be required of every volunteer and staff person.

## 3.3B APPROPRIATE STEPS AFTER A YOUTH MINISTER'S MISCONDUCT

**If the sexual misconduct is with a minor, the church has no choice but to notify the police.** This must be done within 24 hours from when you find out about an allegation—even if everyone believes the accused is innocent. The church can and should inform the accused that the law requires such notification, and it has no bearing on whether the church believes the accused is innocent or guilty. The church also needs to be prepared if an arrest is made. The church should notify legal counsel, denominational leaders, and its insurance company forewarning of the litigious nature of the incident. Many insurance companies cover the costs incurred by the church if their staff members are involved in civil suits. Insurance companies may also cover costs if staff members face criminal charges, but many times this provision isn't made available. Many churches have been caught without coverage because of this discrepancy. Before a situation develops, check with your insurance company to find out what provisions it will make.

**The church should never conduct its own investigation.** The response team can minister to the appropriate parties, but its job isn't to conduct a fact-finding mission. If there are victims from separate families, the church should not bring them together. Many times the police and legal counsel will caution your response team members to not talk about the incident at all.

**While the church shouldn't investigate the facts of the incident, the church can and should investigate to see if there are other victims.** This can be done through a point person who fields calls from families. The church can also give anyone the opportunity to talk with a counselor (perhaps one who's on retainer with the church). Other victims usually come forward in a counseling setting.

**The church should act in a timely manner to inform the church body.** This should be carried out through reading a prepared statement. The statement should be honest and straightforward enough to give people knowledge of what is happening. For example you can say, "In the past few days we came to find out that Pastor X has been accused of sexual misconduct with a teenager in our youth ministry." Never give names or genders of victims and keep the details of the type of sexual misconduct in confidence. Avoid using emotionally charged words such as violated, homosexual, forced, etc. Avoid casting judgment or giving any impression of guilt or innocence. The statement should also note that the police are investigating and an arrest has been made. Inform the church this will be a difficult time and ask for prayer for the victim(s) and their families, for the accused and his family, and for the church response team and leadership as they deal with the situation. Make it clear the church leadership won't talk about specifics, facts, or details. The church must be in a legal position—and foremost, in a spiritual position—to be a sanctuary for all involved. The statement should also include some instructions for the church members:

1. Please don't contact the accused or the accused's family. Any needs should be handled by the response team. Some congregants may say the church should break contact with the accused. Legal counsel may also advise this. But this is where our theology and Christian character must take precedence. Jesus said we should care for the hurting—the widowed and orphans—and minister to those in prison. The accused's spouse and children will be without a family member through this ordeal (and longer if there's a conviction). In addition, the spouse of a convicted offender struggles through a very different kind of pain. Many times that spouse is faced with deciding whether to stay in the relationship or divorce. If the

accused incurs legal fees, the spouse may not be able to afford them. However, the church's insurance may provide coverage for therapy or trauma response.

2. Allow church members to serve the victim's family from a distance (i.e., without knowing who they are) through the proper response person. The church members could bring meals to the church, for example, and the response team or staff could take those to all parties involved.

3. Caution the congregation from attempting to find out details, and from spreading or listening to gossip, rumors, or stories. Even if some people know the facts, they should keep them confidential. Also warn them not to talk to the media. If anyone from the media approaches a congregant for a comment, that church member should say nothing. Instruct congregants to instead point media in the direction of the appropriate response team member.

4. Encourage congregants to talk to counselors to work through this tough time. Be aware tragedy surfaces despair, anger, depression, and hopelessness in people's lives. They may express rage against the church for some grudge they've held for years. They may feel the desperation of a marriage falling apart. They may believe that their teen will be scarred for life, distrust church leaders, or blame a teen's rebellion on the church. A qualified counselor will be able to deal with this appropriately.

5. Let parents know that you'll read the same response to teens at youth group. Do this the next time youth group meets

following the disclosure to the church. Tell parents you'll field questions but cannot talk about the details; encourage parents they should also anticipate questions and answer them appropriately.

6. After reading this statement, field questions from the church body. Don't answer questions that would reveal any details of the incident. If those questions are asked, graciously decline and explain why you cannot answer the questions. Anticipate your response to some of these questions:

- Will there be a lawsuit? Is the church going to be held responsible? Did the church violate any laws or do anything wrong? Have legal counsel brief you in advance on how to answer these.

- How did this happen? Were there any warning signs? Could the church have done anything to prevent this? Remind them thorough background and reference checks are done on all who work with youth and children.

- How will the church care for the victim and the offender? Remember there will be loyalties to all parties involved. Have a brief plan—even if it means saying the church is committed to be a place of healing, which means it's committed to minister to everyone involved.

- What will happen to the teens in our youth ministry? Assure congregants of the church's commitment to make sure teens are immediately cared for and protected. Inform them of ways you'll provide support for teens during this crisis. Also let them know that church life will continue with as little disruption as possible, and that teens will be ministered to effectively.

- When talking to teenagers about the incident, have a clear idea of what the future of the youth ministry will hold. They may ask if the summer missions trip will still happen or who'll be teaching on youth group night. Be ready for that. Be prepared for a very emotional night for teens, even if they've already heard the news. Have counselors available. Encourage teens to pray together. Assure them God will bring the church through this crisis.

Always appoint an interim youth minister after the incident. Sexual misconduct doesn't just affect the families of the victims; it affects all families with teens in that ministry. Families may feel a violation of trust. If an interim is not in place and the church quickly hires another youth pastor, that person is being set up to fail. Families may unintentionally sabotage the ministry and relational connections the new leader tries to build with the teens. Following a youth leader's misconduct, families often become overprotective of their teens, overanalyzing ministry programs and viewing actions of leadership with suspicion.

But if families know that the person stepping in will be interim for at least two years (a time span I strongly recommend), they're more gracious and can work through the trust issues before a new youth pastor takes the helm. Interim youth pastors can be denominational youth workers, professors of youth ministry who can fill in part time, or area parachurch youth workers (e.g., Youth for Christ, Young Life, Fellowship of Christian Athletes, etc.). Many parachurch youth workers raise support and struggle financially —and this invitation could serve them as well for the time of the interim.

The church has a responsibility to bring restoration to the victim and the offender. For both this process should include counseling, pastoral care, spiritual direction, ongoing account-ability for continued growth, healthy fellowship, and encourage-ment to realize a new sense of hope, healing, joy, and abundant life. All need to see that God is bigger than any sin, evil, pain, or suffering anyone could experience.

The church may later be involved in a denominational investiga-tion that will consider the status or discipline of the offender (some denominations strip offenders of their ordinations and more). It may also take a careful look at enacting preventive measures, including changing or formulating new policies and procedures. This investigation should be done after all legal proceedings have been completed and as the church's legal counsel advises.

Churches can also take some preventive measures to keep their staff members healthy. These measures don't necessarily involve creating more policies. While we need regulations for people who work with minors, policies or regulations don't keep offenders from sexual misconduct. Preventative measures should include the following:

**The amount of time and intensity of activity placed upon staff members should be guarded.** Staffers need time for fun and rec-reation. Churches should be more like a family and less like a busi-ness. Care of staff should be more critical than performance.

**Church staffers should be required to meet regularly (every other month) with a spiritual director.** This person should be outside the church, which will allow the spiritual director to focus attention on the staff members without the bias of the work of the church. This will also allow the staff members freedom to talk honestly through struggles.

**Church staffers should be encouraged to maintain a healthy network of friends inside and outside of the church.** Christian friends from other churches allow staffers greater perspective in regard to what God's doing somewhere else and to be more candid. In addition, staffers should make a point to not talk about work when they're with their circle of friends. Often church workers tend to talk only about ministry. As mentioned previously, staffers' networks of close friends shouldn't include teens.

**Staffers should be encouraged and held accountable for their personal and spiritual growth.** As soon as supervisors prescribe this (e.g., "Our entire staff will read the following book for growth," etc.), it becomes work. Instead the accountability should surround asking about what they're reading, or what actions they are taking for growth (this can range from taking a dance class to doing a personal study of Lamentations). Other accountability questions can include, "How is this helping you grow as a person? Spiritually? Why did you choose to read that book...take that class... engage in that event, etc.? What do you hope to accomplish? Have you done that? What can this church be doing to help you and your family stay healthy and grow?"

**Two staff meetings per year should be designated for each staff member to verbalize their passions and joys in ministry.** While this exercise can result in very positive outcomes and should be done regularly, many times it reveals the unhealthy obsessions youth workers can develop. If a staff member is passionate about seeing one particular teen rescued, that passion may be demanding far too much unhealthy time. Equally, if a staff member is lacking joy, that staffer is in a very vulnerable place. Those holding the staffers accountable have a great responsibility to walk with those staffers into joy.

**Ultimately, if we want to ensure our church leaders are healthy, we need to make the church a safe place for us to be ourselves and share our struggles.** Unfortunately, too many churches are guided by business principles from corporate America. This creates an environment in which staffers feel as though they're constantly being evaluated for performance and must be guarded about their real feelings in order to protect their jobs. The result is that staffers won't say what they're really thinking, feeling, or doing for fear of being fired. The church can't operate as a corporation and be healthy. It must be a family in which staffers know they won't be abandoned in their struggles, put away, abused, but rather loved, nurtured, cared for, and developed for the long haul.

## 3.4 TIPS FOR PARENTS ON DISCIPLINING TEENAGERS
Disciplining teenagers is hard work. Many people who are abusive believe they're appropriately disciplining their teens. I read an article once in which the writer believed that teenagers should be disciplined with a literal rod, as Proverbs notes. The writer had pictures and measurements of how a wooden rod would most resemble a "biblical" rod. The main premise was it's okay to beat teenagers with wooden rods as long as you love them.

Not surprisingly, there are better principles that should inform how we discipline teenagers. Here are a few:

- Listen to your teens.
- Don't respond when you're angry. You have time. If the confrontation escalates, call a timeout so things aren't said in anger.
- Make sure the consequence appropriately fits the inappropriate behavior.
- Reason with them rather than berating them.
- Set realistic boundaries and remain consistent.
- Remember you're a parent, not a buddy.
- Stick to the script—make sure you deal with your teen's inappropriate actions. This isn't a time to tell your teens about everything you believe is wrong with their character or lifestyle.
- Don't pass things off as "normal teenage behavior," even if consistent discipline (coaching) is required.
- Don't air your dirty laundry by saying things like, "I did that when I was your age, and now I regret it." The thought-response of a smart teenager would be, "You did it, and you turned out okay—maybe I won't regret it."
- Don't prevent your teens from feeling the natural consequences of their actions.
- Praise and reward appropriate behavior.

## 3.5 TIPS ON DEALING WITH DATING VIOLENCE

Dating violence will likely be present in your youth ministry. As a preventive measure, youth workers should raise teens' and parents' awareness about the issue and encourage teens to avoid becoming part of abusive relationships or tolerating them if their friends are in them. In remedying the problem you can do the following:

## 3.5A TIPS FOR PARENTS

**If you have suspicions about the health of your teen's relationship, give your teen an opportunity to talk.** Ask nonthreatening questions about how things are going—the best thing about the relationship, etc. Then just listen. If your teen is unresponsive, don't press the issue but come back to it at a later date. This will let your teen know that you really care.

**Have a general conversation about relational abuse and the warning signs.** Teach your teen she should have expectations from a boyfriend that include mutual love and respect, the desire to see the other flourish, commitment to each other's success, valuing each other's families, respect for familial boundaries and rules, and a respect for parental authority, and to have respect for oneself (i.e., that neither person in the relationship should ever condone being dominated, pushed around, degraded, or mistreated).

**Don't let your teen keep a computer in his room. If there's public or limited computer access, your teen won't likely be coerced into all-night chat sessions.** This helps the teen keep healthier boundaries.

**Create boundaries around cell phone use. Perhaps after 11 p.m. all family cell phones are placed in a central location for recharging.** No calls come in or go out. Teens who are being manipulated by a dating partner are likely afraid or cannot break free from the long hours they're held hostage on the phone by their partners. This rule helps gives your teen a way of escape.

**Set limits on the amount of time your teen can spend with his or her dating partner.** Consider a positive, rather than a negative, approach to this. For example, don't tell your teen she can't spend time with the boyfriend; instead tell your teen she must spend at least two nights with family per week. During this family time, cell phones are shut off in order to focus on time together. In addition, plan things such as going to lunch or a movie with just you and your teen.

**If you have suspicions the relationship is abusive, confront your teen, reassuring her that you're there to help and not to pass judgment.** Keep the focus on loving and supporting your teen, not on bad-mouthing the girlfriend. Remember that your teen may still have strong feelings and loyalties toward that person, and showing anger may enmesh the teen deeper in commitment to the dating relationship. By focusing on your teen, you can identify your observations of how he has changed, the lack of joy you see in the relationship, and the appearance of being trapped by long, exhausting conversations, etc.

**If your teen comes home with bruises, wounds, etc., notify the authorities.** That said, parents should never threaten the boyfriend. You must remember you're also dealing with a minor and there are consequences if you react physically or make threats. You may have to arrange to have your teen stay for a few days with friends or relatives to get her away from the abusive partner.

**Notify the school so lockers and class schedules can be changed.** Notifying the school can also be a security measure so officials can keep a watchful eye on the abuser.

## 3.5B HELPING TEENS BREAK FREE FROM ABUSIVE DATING RELATIONSHIPS

**Breaking free from an abuser is never easy for victims—even after they realize how abusive their situations are.** Many fear retaliation or being alone without dating partners, or they second-guess their decisions. It's likely their dating partners had become a big part of their lives and identities, and without them things may not feel normal.

**Remind teens it's normal they may miss their exes, but that doesn't mean they made bad decisions, or that they should get back together.** Often victims stay in an abusive relationship because they love the security or status relationships can provide more than they love the other person in the relationship.

**Have teens rehearse what they'll say when they break up.** This is important because the more they rehearse, the more difficult it will be for the exes to manipulate them. Rehearsal can also give teens more confidence.

**If teens feel as though they'll be in harm's way, encourage them to have friends present.** Breaking up with violent abusers should always be done in public (e.g., a fast-food place is ideal). The accompanying friends may either be at the victim's side or visible to the victim and abuser, somewhere in that public setting (e.g., sitting at another table in the venue). Ideally a parent or another caring adult should be present. A public setting should keep the abuser from becoming violent. The support person's visibility should prevent the abuser from becoming manipulative and controlling.

**Encourage teens to have a plan that can get them to safety.** This should include memorizing phone numbers of friends or family members they can call (most teens store numbers in their cell phones and do not know them by heart). If they're unable to use their cell phones, it puts them in another vulnerable situation.

**If teens are too fearful to face their exes, they should break up over the phone.** While this is poor etiquette, in this circumstance it may be the best option. Abusive patterns may warrant that the break-up be done this way to increase safety. The teen should be coached to say that this was the only way to break up considering the other person's violent patterns. Even if teens break up over the phone, they should rehearse what will be said and should have a friend or adult present for support.

**Make sure teens set time limits on the conversations. Remind them long, drawn-out conversations are forms of control and manipulation.** The sheer exhaustion created by hours of conversation can cause victims to cave. The victims should know they don't have to convince exes of the reasons for breaking up; it's likely no reasons will be good enough to satisfy the abusers, who'll twist reasons, cast blame for problems on the victims, and confuse the victims. It's good for the support people to also be timekeepers. If the agreed-upon time limit is up, the support person should step in and rescue. It's also good to have an "out" plan, meaning the victims and support persons should schedule to meet with someone else just after the breakup meeting. There's an unquestionable authority among teens when they hear phrases such as "I'm supposed to meet my parents at 9 p.m." If parents are the support people, just saying, "Its time to go now" is authoritative enough.

Make sure the abused teens anticipate some of the manipulative responses that the exes may use: Promises of change, threats of harm, death, or suicide, or threats of humiliating the victim. When threats start, it's time to walk away.

Tell victims to not answer the phone, respond to the texts, or even open emails from abusers after breakups. Remember abusers aren't operating like normal teenagers. Not responsding must be a boundary that helps enable and empower victims from being further victimized.

Encourage victims to tell as many people as possible that the relationship is over. It's important to have many support people aware of the abusive nature of the relationship. Parents, teachers, coaches, youth workers, and others in authority should become part of that network.

Encourage victims to avoid isolated areas where exes could confront them. Prior to breaking up it may be strategic to have plans to travel to and from school, work, etc. with friends and/ or always have a group of friends to eat lunch with, study with in the library, go into restrooms with, etc. There is strength in numbers.

If exes come to victims' houses when parents aren't home, the victims shouldn't open the doors. If victims fear being at school, school counselors should be notified so action can be taken to increase safety.

Save all threatening messages and emails. In some cases changing cell phone numbers, getting new email addresses, and setting social network profiles to private may be appropriate actions.

Stalking is a form of terrorizing, intimidating, frightening, harassing, and threatening an individual. Stalking is illegal. If this occurs, notify the police. The victims should call 911 if they sense imminent danger.

## 3.5C EDUCATING TEENS TO RECOGNIZE WARNING SIGNS REGARDING DATING VIOLENCE

From the statistics recorded in the first section of this book, you can see that many teens have had or are in abusive relationships. Many more know others in abusive relationships. This is a very current issue that needs to be addressed in youth ministry and in the community. Your youth ministry can help decrease dating violence in your community. Here are some ways to educate teenagers:

- Make all adolescents aware of dating violence and the warning signs.
- Challenge youth to privately talk to friends they believe are in abusive relationships. Make sure they identify the warning signs (e.g., name-calling, put-downs, physical aggression, controlling behavior, changes in abused friends' behavior, etc.).
- Your teens should challenge their friends to call helplines so they can talk, ask questions, and get advice anonymously. The Love Is Respect National Dating Violence Helpline number is 866-331-9474.
- Tell teens to challenge their friends to talk to adults who can help (e.g., counselors, teachers, parents, adult volunteers in the youth ministry or church, etc.).
- Tell your teens not to bash their friends' abusers out of relationship loyalty; instead, they should focus on the care of

their friends. Also, your teens shouldn't give ultimatums to their abused friends (e.g., "If you continue to date that person, then we can't be friends" or, "If you don't talk to your dating partner about how horrible you're being treated, then I will"). Abused teens are threatened enough. Presented with an ultimatum, they'll likely choose to stay in the relationship.

- Teach teenage guys that aggressiveness and dominance in a relationship are unacceptable and not at all manly. Guys need to build reputations of treating females with kindness and respect.
- Let teens know that if partners in relationships demand intimacy, sex, or anything else, they should end the relationship.
- Teach girls that verbal attacks, gossip, and rumor-spreading are abusive behavior.
- Tell teens jealousy and possessiveness aren't signs of romance, deep love, or concern for the relationship. These are self-focused actions.
- Teens should understand that Christ calls them to be loving, respectful servants who think of others as more important than themselves. Those characteristics mark healthy friendships and healthy dating relationships.

## 3.5D HELPING ABUSERS AND ABUSED FAMILIES

The church has been entrusted with the mandate to be God's agents of reconciliation and restoration in people's lives. Therefore the church has a responsibility to assist families in their journeys toward becoming whole. That means we have a responsibility to abusers as much as we do the victims. The starting place is to develop an understanding of how we should balance healing to victims and restoration of abusers. Helping both the families of abused teens and of abusers of those teens is no small or quick action. It's very time-intensive and people-intensive. It demands that quality people come around families to nurture, develop, and disciple them for a lifetime. Here are some tips:

- First and foremost make sure the family is safe. This may require that family members stay with others in the congregation for a period of time. Help the abuser understand that help is available. As soon as the abuser is removed from the home, the family can resume living there.

- There are often legal repercussions for physical and sexual abuse of minors. The legal recourse is greater against sexual abusers. This may often fragment families as minors end up in foster care, parents are incarcerated, and other family members are left in limbo. The church should assign leaders to minister care to all involved, attending to the family's needs and serving as the agents who give stability and consistency to the family.

- Build a support team around the nonabusive parent. This team should consist of people who have pastoral care gifts or gifts of hospitality, and who can mobilize resources. This team becomes the primary caregivers to assess the needs and progress of the family. Do the same for the abuser—even if the abuser is incarcerated. Continual visits, accountability, love, and encouragement may help bring the abuser into right relationship with God, family, and friends.

- Remember that the family may face financial difficulties, especially if the abuser is the primary provider. The church should be ready to use benevolence funds to help cover some family expenses and be willing to provide meals and other services. Members of the congregation who are medical doctors, lawyers, and mental health professionals may be encouraged to offer counsel and support without cost.

- In advance the church should consider challenging members of the congregation to become certified foster parents. When family problems arise within the church, these people can minister to minors without taking them out of the school or church.

- Refer the family to professional counselors and work in a support role with therapists. In an abusive situation, churches should rely on trained clinicians to provide counseling, and focus instead on serving the family members' daily needs.

# Resources for Helping Teenagers Who Encounter Abuse

| Section 4 |

## 4.1A AGENCIES

**National Sexual Violence Resource Center**
123 North Enola Drive, Enola, PA 17025
Toll-free: 877-739-3895
www.nsvrc.org

**National Center for Victims of Crime**
2000 M Street NW, Suite 480, Washington, DC 20036
Phone: 202-467-8700
Helpline: 800-FYI-CALL (800-394-2255): the helpline is staffed
Monday through Friday from 8:30 a.m. to 8:30 p.m. EST.
email: gethelp@NCVC.org
www.ncvc.org

**Childhelp**
15757 N. 78th Street, Scottsdale, Arizona 85206
Phone: 480-922-8212
http://www.childhelp.org/2009/home

## Crisis and Reporting Hotlines

### National Teen Dating Abuse Help
866-331-9474
A 24-hour crisis line for teenagers in abusive relationships. Teen callers can remain anonymous.

### National Runaway Switchboard
800-621-4000
This 24-hour hotline is a referral service for youth in personal crisis and/or adults who need to report or seek guidance regarding runaway teens.

### State Protective Service Report Hotlines
Some states are divided into regions and don't have a central number, or they give central numbers that will direct you to agencies within your region. For states without 24-hour hotlines, it may mean that calls are taken through the local police department in collaboration with the state's child protective services.

- Alabama: Call 800-4-A-CHILD for assistance
- Alaska: 800-478-4444
- Arizona: 888-SOS-CHILD (888-767-2443)
- Arkansas: 800-482-5964
- California: Call 800-4-A-CHILD for assistance
- Colorado: Call 800-4-A-CHILD for assistance
- Connecticut: 800-842-2288
- Delaware: 800-292-9582
- District of Columbia: 877-671-SAFE (877-671-7233)
- Florida: 800-96-ABUSE (800-962-2873)
- Georgia: Call 800-4-A-CHILD for assistance
- Hawaii: 800-832-5300 (Oahu); other islands call 800-4-A-CHILD for assistance

- Idaho: 800-926-2588
- Illinois: 800-25ABUSE (800-252-2873)
- Indiana: 800-800-5556
- Iowa: 800-362-2178
- Kansas: 800-922-5330
- Kentucky: 800-752-6200
- Louisiana: 225-342-6832
- Maine: 800-452-1999
- Maryland: 800-332-6347 is the report hotline but not available 24 hours.
- Massachusetts: 800-792-5200
- Michigan: 800-942-4357
- Minnesota: 651-291-0211
- Mississippi: 800-222-8000
- Missouri: 800-392-3738 or 573-751-3448
- Montana: 866-820-KIDS (866-820-5437)
- Nebraska: 800-652-1999
- Nevada: 800-992-5757 or 775-684-4400
- New Hampshire: 800-894-5533 or 603-271-6556; lines available 8 a.m. to 4:30 p.m., Monday through Friday
- New Jersey: 800-652-2873
- New Mexico: 800-797-3260
- New York: 800-342-3720
- North Carolina: Call 800-4-A-CHILD for assistance
- North Dakota: 800-245-3736 or 701-328-2316
- Ohio: Call 800-4-A-CHILD for assistance
- Oklahoma: 800-522-3511
- Oregon: Call 800-4-A-CHILD for assistance
- Pennsylvania: 800-932-0313
- Rhode Island: 800-RI-CHILD (800-742-4453)
- South Carolina: 803-898-7318
- South Dakota: Call 800-4-A-CHILD for assistance
- Tennessee: 877-237-0004
- Texas: 800-252-5400
- Utah: 800-678-9399 will connect you to a number in your area

- Vermont: 800-649-5285
- Virginia: 800-552-7096 or 804-786-8536
- Washington: 866-END-HARM (866-363-4276)
- West Virginia: 800-352-6513
- Wisconsin: Call local police
- Wyoming: 800-457-3659

**National Child Abuse Hotline**
800-4-A-CHILD (800-422-4453) or
800-2-A-CHILD (800-222-4453)
If you cannot reach your state or local agency, call this hotline.

## 4.2 ONLINE RESOURCES

**Child Welfare Information Gateway**
This Web site allows you to search for statutes and mandatory reporting requirements by state.
http://www.childwelfare.gov/systemwide/laws_policies/state/

**National Youth Violence Prevention Resource Center**
A federal resource for communities working to prevent violence committed by and against young people. The mission of the NYVPRC is to provide key leaders in communities—local government leaders and community leaders—with dynamic resources to help support their efforts to plan, develop, implement, and evaluate effective youth violence prevention efforts.
http://www.safeyouth.org/scripts/index.asp

## Support for Male Sex-Abuse Victims

There are many organizations that have been established to help male survivors of sexual abuse. Many of them are not uniquely Christian but serve to bring healing to wounded male sex-abuse victims (there are no Christian ministries for male sexual-abuse survivors—that should tell us something). The following web sites present a very comprehensive understanding of male sexual abuse and can clarify a lot of questions that a male survivor may have:

- **1 in 6: Courage, Hope & Strength:** Their mission is to help men who've had unwanted or abusive sexual experiences in childhood live healthier, happier lives. http://www.1in6.org/HOME/tabid/36/Default.aspx
- **Male Survivor:** Committed to preventing, healing, and eliminating all forms of sexual victimization of boys and men through support, treatment, research, education, advocacy, and activism. http://www.malesurvivor.org/default.html

### The National Center for Missing and Exploited Children
This is an informative website with links and information for anyone involved in preventing abuse. The section for parents and guardians is especially helpful with tips to help keep your child safer. **http://www.missingkids.com**

## 4.3 BOOKS AND PRINTED MATERIAL

*Teen Action Toolkit: Building a Youth-Led Response to Teen Victimization.* This resource was developed by the Department of Justice and the National Center for Victims of Crime. It's a hands-on implementation guide for the Teen Action Partnership for Teen Victims program that marshals the strengths of youth as leaders to transform their communities' responses to teenage victims of crime while building the resilience of the youth participants at the same time. This free, 168-page program includes a step-by-step guide to setting up the program, exercises, handouts, and resources. It can be downloaded at http://www.ncvc.org/tvp/AGP.Net/Components/Document-Viewer/Download.aspxnz?DocumentID=43492

# Notes

1. Dean Kilpatrick, PhD, and Benjamin Saunders, PhD, "The Prevalence and Consequences of Child Victimization," *National Institutes of Justice Research Preview*, U.S. Department of Justice, April 1997.

2. http://www.acf.hhs.gov/programs/cb/laws_policies/cblaws/capta/index.htm

3. http://www.ojp.usdoj.gov/bjs/pub/pdf/apvsvc.pdf

4. http://www.acf.hhs.gov/programs/cb/pubs/cm06/chapter3.htm#noteseven

5. http://www.acf.hhs.gov/programs/cb/pubs/cm06/chapter4.htm

6. *Child Maltreatment 2006*: http://www.acf.hhs.gov/programs/cb/pubs/cm06/chapter3.htm#noteseven

7. http://www.childhelpusa.org/resources/learning-center/statistics

8. Ibid.

9. http://www.brycs.org/brycs_spotapr2005.pdf

10. Tom McIntyre and Patricia Silva, *Beyond Behavior* (1992), volume 4, no. 1 (1992): 8–12.

11. Miguel De La Torre is the assistant professor of religion at Hope College. His book *Santeria: The Beliefs and Rituals of a Growing Religion in America* (published by Eerdmans) gives more insight into this growing practice.

12. The U.S. Department of Justice (March 3, 1996; 202/307-0784) released data indicating that two-thirds of sexual offenders in state prisons had been sexually abused as children. See http://www.ojp.usdoj.gov/bjs/pub/press/cvvoatv.pr. In 1999 the Department of Justice stated that 36 percent of all women incarcerated in U.S. jails and 14 percent of all men had been abused as children. See U.S. Department of Justice, *Prior Abuse Reported by Inmates*

and *Probationers* (1999; 202/307-0784) http://www.ojp.gov/bjs/abstract/parip. htm. Church leaders must be careful to not twist statistics and make sure the sources of statistics are credible.

13. For more information on teenagers and homosexuality, see *What Do I Do When... Teenagers Question Their Sexuality?* in this book series.

14. http://www.acf.hhs.gov/programs/cb/pubs/cm07/chapter5.htm

15. Ibid.

16. http://www.apa.org/releases/sexabuse/perpetrators.html

17. For more information on teenagers and violence outside of the home, see *What Do I Do When... Teenagers Encounter Bullying and Violence?* in this book series.

18. http://ojp.usdoj.gov/bjs/pub/press/fvspr.htm

19. http://www.stopfamilyviolence.org/info/custody-abuse/statistics/10-custody-myths-and-how-to-counter-them

20. http://www.1800runaway.org/news_events/third.html

21. http://www.cdc.gov/violenceprevention/intimatepartnerviolence/datingvio lence.html

22. C. T. Halpern, et al, "Partner violence among adolescents in opposite-sex romantic relationships: Findings from the national longitudinal study of adolescent health," *American Journal of Public Health*, 2001, 91(10): 1679-85.

23. Sarah Avery-Leaf and Michele Cascardi, *Dating Violence Education: Prevention and Early Intervention Strategies in Preventing Violence in Relationships* (Paul A. Schewe, ed., 2002), 82.

24. http://www.cdc.gov/mmwr/PDF/ss/ss5104.pdf

25. C. Molidor, and R. M. Tolman, "Gender and contextual factors in adolescent dating violence," *Violence Against Women*, 1998, 4, 180-94.

26. V. A Foshee, G. F. Linder, K. E. Bauman, et al. "The Safe Dates Project: theoretical basis, evaluation design, and selected baseline findings," *American Journal of Preventive Medicine* 1996, 12(2): 39-47.

27. http://www.cdc.gov/mmwr/preview/mmwrhtml/mm5519a3.htm

28. Ibid.

29. L. L. Kupper, et al., "Prevalence of Partner Violence in Same-Sex Romantic and Sexual Relationships in a National Sample of Adolescents," *Journal of Adolescent Health* 35 (2004): 124-31.

30. J. Greene, "Youth with Runaway, Throwaway, and Homeless Experiences: Prevalence, Drug Use, and Other At-Risk Behaviors," *Research Triangle Institute,* HHS, ACF - ACYF 1995.

31. B. Molnar, S. Shade, A. Kral, R. Booth, and J. Watters, "Suicidal Behavior and Sexual/Physical Abuse Among Street Youth," *Child Abuse and Neglect.* no. 3 (1998): 213-22.

32. H. Hammer, D. Finkelhor, and A. Sedlak, "Runaway/Throwaway Children: National Estimates and Characteristics." National Incidence Studies of Missing, Abducted, Runaway, and Throwaway Children. Office of Juvenile Justice and Delinquency Prevention (2002).

33. http://www.acf.hhs.gov/programs/cb/laws_policies/cblaws/capta/capta1.htm#111

34. http://www.usdoj.gov/criminal/ceos/prostitution.html

35. Table 1 at http://www.ojp.usdoj.gov/bjs/pub/pdf/saycrle.pdf

36. Centers for Disease Control, Adverse Childhood Experience Study. See results at http://www.cdc.gov/nccdphp/ace/prevalence.htm. Realize that this is a conservative statistic based on people who are reporting. The figure may actually be higher because many victims, especially guys, rarely report being victimized.

37. Others are victimized by people they know and trust, and depending on how the researchers define incest, that may include extended family members. This being true, the percentage of sexual abuse within familial contexts may be greater. See D. Kilpatrick, B. Saunders, and D. Smith, "Youth Victimization: Prevalence and Implications," U.S. Department of Justice, National Institute of Justice report (2003).

38. Wisconsin Subcommittee on Adolescent Pregnancy Prevention. Department of Health and Family Services, 1998. See http://www.wcasa.org/docs/teen.pdf

39. http://www.cdc.gov/ncipc/dvp/SV/SVDataSheet.pdf

40. http://www.usdoj.gov/ag/readingroom/drugcrime.htm

41. This complex issue of sexual identity is more thoroughly explored in my book, *Teenage Guys: Exploring Issues Adolescent Guys Face and the Strategies to Help Them* (Youth Specialties/Zondervan).

42. http://www.cdc.gov/nccdphp/ace/prevalence.htm

43. S. R. Dube, R. F. Anda, C. L. Whitfield, et al., "Long-term consequences of childhood sexual abuse by gender of victim," *American Journal of Preventive Medicine* 28 (2005): 430-438.

44. National Institute of Justice & Centers for Disease Control and Prevention, *Prevalence, Incidence and Consequences of Violence Against Women Survey,* 1998. See http://www.ncjrs.gov/pdffiles/172837.pdf

45. D. Lisak, J. Hopper, and P. Song, "Factors in the cycle of violence: Gender rigidity and emotional constriction." *Journal of Traumatic Stress* 9 (1996): 721-43.

46. T. Blackwell, "Academics see sex crimes in schoolyard," *The National Post (May 2002)*

47. http://www.phac-aspc.gc.ca/ncfv-cnivf/pdfs/invisib.pdf

48. National Center for the Victims of Crime. See http://www.ncvc.org/ncvc/main.aspx?dbName=DocumentViewer&DocumentID=32361

49. See Child help; http://www.childhelp.org/resources/learning-center/following-simple-rules/misconceptions

50. As defined by the state of New York. See http://www.nyc.gov/html/acs/html/child_safety/mandated_reporters.shtml

In this series of books designed for anyone connected to teenagers, Dr. Steven Gerali addresses six daunting and difficult situations that, when they do happen, often leave youth workers and parents feeling unprepared. With a background in adolescent counseling, Dr. Gerali provides valuable resources to help youth workers and parents through some of the most challenging situations they may face.

Each book defines the issue, explores how different theological perspectives can impact the situation, offers helpful, practical tips, along with credible resources to help readers go deeper into the issues they're dealing with.

*What Do I Do When Teenagers Encounter Bullying and Violence?*
978-0-310-29194-7

*What Do I Do When Teenagers Deal with Death?*
978-0-310-29193-0

*What Do I Do When Teenagers Are Victims of Abuse?*
978-0-310-29195-4

*What Do I Do When Teenagers Are Depressed and Contemplate Suicide?*
978-0-310-29196-1

*What Do I Do When Teenagers Struggle with Eating Disorders?*
978-0-310-29197-8

*What Do I Do When Teenagers Question Their Sexuality?*
978-0-310-29198-5

Dr. Steven Gerali
Retail $6.99 each

Visit www.youthspecialties.com
or your local bookstore

youth
specialties

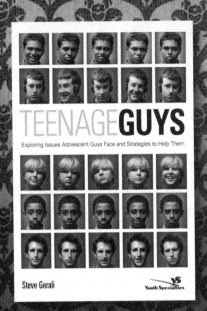

In *Teenage Guys*, author Steve Gerali breaks down the stages of development that adolescent guys go through, providing stories from his own experiences in ministry and counseling, as well as practical research findings to equip youth workers (both male and female) to more effectively minister to teenage guys. Each chapter includes advice from counselors and veteran youth workers, as well as discussion questions.

### Teenage Guys
*Exploring Issues Adolescent Guys Face and Strategies to Help Them*

Steve Gerali
Retail $17.99
978-0-310-26985-4

Visit www.youthspecialties.com
or your local bookstore.